THE RIGH
INTERPRET YOUR DREAMS

In the same series:

The Right Way to Read Music
Stop Bingeing!
The New A-Z of Babies' Names

All uniform with this book

THE RIGHT WAY TO INTERPRET YOUR DREAMS

Dr Elizabeth Scott

Whilst care is taken in selecting Authors who are authoritative in their subjects, it is emphasised that their books can reflect their knowledge only up to the time of writing. Information can be superseded and printers' errors can creep in. This book is sold, therefore, on the condition that neither Publisher nor Author can be held legally responsible for the consequences of any error or omission there may be.

Typeset in 11/13pt Times by Letterpart Ltd., Reigate, Surrey.

Printed and bound in Great Britain by Cox & Wyman Ltd., Reading, Berkshire.

The *Right Way* series is published by Elliot Right Way Books, Brighton Road, Lower Kingswood, Tadworth, Surrey, KT20 6TD, U.K. For information about our company and the other books we publish, visit our website at www.right-way.co.uk

CONTENTS

ACKNOWLEDGEMENTS

I should like to thank Dr Derek Ball, Consultant Psychiatrist, for his helpful advice and all those friends and patients who allowed me to use their dreams.

INTRODUCTION

Forget Freud

When it comes to dream interpretation, you are the person best equipped to make sense of your dreams. No one knows better where each dream picture comes from or what it means to you. Dreams are personal things. They come from *your* brain and they are as they are because of who you have become or what you are wanting, doing or worrying about. The pictures they show you come from how and where you live and what you have experienced in life, literature or visual experiences such as television.

The best that dream analysts can do is to help you to take your dreams apart, encourage you to select what is important and meaningful, and discuss your waking feelings about your incredible night adventures.

Because analysts have come from a different upbringing from you, their own reaction to your dream picture may lead them astray so that you end up with an analysis of what *they* feel about your dream. You may even be too embarrassed to describe fully a dream whose content seems out of character for the sort of person you like to think you are. Your dream analyst then has only half a picture to work on.

This is where this book may help. It will show you how to

work out your own dream analysis and how to profit from these night pictures that you conjure up.

Who dreams?

Some people say that they scarcely dream at all. It may be so, but unless they are taking medication that suppresses Rapid Eye Movement sleep (the most common time for dreams to be experienced), or have some serious disturbance of sleep pattern, the odds are that they are experiencing dreams but not remembering them. This is not as unusual as it seems because you have to wake immediately after a dream, or in the middle of a dream, to become aware of it. Most dreams have an evanescence that is quite extraordinary. Wake to a dream and get up, go to the bathroom and come back, and you will usually find you can't remember any of it unless you have jotted down a few reminders as soon as you wake. This appears to be a normal body function. You only remember the dreams that really matter. It is unlike encounters with people by day when quite casual meetings can be recalled, perhaps even years later.

The importance of dreaming

Since the first man dreamed a dream, curled round in his cave beside his fire of sticks, and woke and told it to his family, dreams have fascinated men and women. But mostly they enthral only the dreamer. Telling your dream is usually a big yawn to everyone else. It is seldom a story. It doesn't hang together. It is a pastel coloured movie full of meaningless unconnected scenes that are boring and unimpressive to an audience.

You are still overwhelmed by the sights and sounds of your dream, so it is important to you in the morning. You want to share the exciting time you have experienced. Your spouse, your partner, your family or workmates are uninterested. They have had just as good or bad dreams of their own and, unless they know you well enough to make a guess at the reason behind your dream, have no interest in your tale.

The meanings of dreams

I believe that the dreams you remember long enough to tell do have a meaning. I believe they are meant to be acted on. They are, if you like, an early warning system where in dream sleep your brain accepts messages from all over your body, translating them into pictures that, if not sorted out during sleep, are tossed into consciousness like an in-bound memo at the office. At the most simplistic level, who has not dreamed of wandering on and on through bizarre surroundings searching unsuccessfully for a toilet, only to wake needing to urinate?

Not all dreams are that easy to interpret. If you looked back over your night's journey you would find feelings and sights that held clues to your current lifestyle. You might want to explore these further to see if there were other strong feelings highlighted in your dream.

1

AN OVERVIEW OF DREAM INTERPRETATION

Early dream divination

Our ancestors were hooked on dream divination. As early as the time of the Pharaohs, interpreting dreams was a skilled art. In that society it was important enough to be the prerogative of the priests.

Joseph

The Old Testament story of Joseph has survived from religious texts written before 1000 BC. Thrown in to prison by his master, whose wife had wrongly accused him of attempted rape, Joseph's good character and behaviour had allowed him to become the 'trusty' in the jail. He looked after the other prisoners. So, when Pharaoh's butler and baker were consigned to his jail for misdemeanours, Joseph was there to interpret their dreams. It is interesting that, although Joseph listened to the products of their understandably disturbed sleep, he was shy of providing an interpretation, telling them that this was the prerogative of their own priesthood, and that his interpretations were not his own but came from his God. It is clear that at that time dream divination was the province of religious leaders and not in the common domain.

Joseph, however, had experience in interpreting dreams.

When he was seventeen he dreamed that he and his brothers were gathering in their wheat sheaves and their sheaves all bowed to his upright one. His analysis of this got him into real trouble. He told his brothers that it meant that he would be greater than them. Already irritated by the fact that he was their father's favourite son they pitched him in to a pit and then, at a loss how to get rid of him finally without killing him, sold him to a passing caravan of Ishmaelites bound for Egypt, who in turn sold him to Potiphar, his previous master.

However, Pharaoh's butler and baker persuaded him to listen to their dreams. The butler had dreamed that he was standing in front of a vine with three branches which before his eyes had burst into flowers which matured into grapes. The butler had pressed the grapes into Pharaoh's cup and set it in his master's hand. Then he woke.

"The three branches are three days," Joseph told him, "and in three days you will receive a pardon and be holding your master's cup again just as usual."

Heartened by this, the baker said, "I dreamed I had three baskets of cakes for Pharaoh. I was carrying them on my head but the birds were pecking the cakes as I went."

"Again you are looking at three days," interpreted Joseph. "However, within three days Pharaoh will lift up your head from you, hang you from a tree and the birds will peck the flesh from you."

In three days Pharaoh had a birthday and, as was clearly the custom, he pardoned some of the people he had jailed and executed some. Joseph may or may not have been aware of this practice, he probably was. The butler and the baker certainly were and their dreams were very accurate pictures of what they hoped or feared in their heart of hearts. Joseph merely made sense of their feelings for them. That he had a talent for dream interpretation is undoubted.

Joseph went on to interpret Pharaoh's dreams when, faced with mass dissension in the interpretation of them amongst his priests, his butler remembered Joseph, still languishing in jail, and mentioned his prowess to his master.

The Pharaoh dreamed that he was standing on the banks of the Nile and seven cows, fat and sleek, came up from the river and fed in the reeds. They were followed by seven emaciated cows who ate up the fat cows but remained as thin as before. Then he woke.

He also dreamed that he saw seven ears of wheat growing on one stalk, plump and healthy but beside them were seven wizened ears of wheat and they swallowed up the good ears but remained blighted.

Joseph told the Pharaoh that the seven fat cows and the seven plump ears of wheat were seven years of plenty and the scrawny cows and wizened wheat ears were seven years of famine that would follow. He advised stockpiling food in the good years so that the country could outlive the seven years of famine.

What Joseph appreciated was that the Pharaoh was in some way aware that he was seeing the agricultural boom before the bust. Perhaps he had previously seen similar signs of a good harvest preceding a famine, and maybe he was noticing that the summer was getting longer, the wet season shorter. Whatever it was, Pharaoh was very ready to accept that diagnosis and to act on it. By day his mind was full of conflicting thoughts, but by night his brain was isolating an anxiety and showing it to him in picture form. More importantly, showing it to him again and again. Repetitive dreams are more significant than occasional night pictures. Both Pharaoh and Joseph would have been aware of that. It was a time when people really did discuss each other's dreams much as doctors discuss the laboratory results of blood and urine tests today.

Pharaoh may not have wanted to accept the idea of imminent famine. His priests might not want to be the bearers of bad news. But, when he had it put to him, Pharaoh recognised that Joseph had got it right. These apparent dreams of prognostication are not from higher or outside sources. They are usually your own sensitive observations being highlighted during sleep where pointers, unremarked during the day, come together to make a picture. I shall discuss these dreams on page 102.

Egyptian dream divination

There are old Egyptian writings from the millennia before Christ was born, detailing the meanings of dreams:

"If a woman dreams she is having sex with a goat, she is likely to die; with a dog, she will be delivered of a boy; with a cat, she will have many children."

The prognostications from these dreams would make no sense nowadays because the animals arouse different connotations in a modern mind; besides which, dreams of intercourse are still treated as wholly erotic and sexually abnormal in a way they could not have been in early Egypt. At that time, sexual dreams were clearly acceptable happenings that anyone could have and discuss.

The Early Middle East

In the millennia before Christ and the years just after, dreams continued to be thought important. Their interpretation by a process known as incubation, or sleeping in a holy place to obtain dreams from the gods, became the prerogative of priest-doctors throughout Turkey and the Middle East within huge temples built for the purpose.

I visited one such at Palmyra in Syria and it was clear that it had been a thriving organisation. The forecourt where people arrived with their sacrifices, usually goats, was enormous. There was an extensive area for the petitioners to purify themselves in great water tanks, then get on with sacrificing their offerings and petitioning the priests in the high-pillared temple, which dominated the whole. There, overwhelmed by the flickering light of the torches, the sights and sounds of sacrifice, the fog of incense and the clashing music of the priests, they would be submerged in awe and, when wrapped in the skin of their sacrifice and told to sleep, would certainly dream. In the morning the priests would interpret that dream and the pilgrim would be free to return home, happy or sad depending on the outcome, but certainly much impressed.

Ancient Greek philosophy

Plato, a Greek aristocrat, teacher and philosopher writing between 400 and 300 BC to encourage men to live a rational and well-ordered life without excesses, realised that in sleep there lurk anarchic thoughts and physical appetites that are uncontrollable.

Aristotle, writing a little later, likened dreams to the swirls of water in a river as, meeting with obstruction, they continually divide and change course. His questions of why you dream and why you fail to remember your dreams are only recently finding answers.

Gradually the priests lost power and scientific thinking began to invade therapeutic practices. Pliny the Elder, a Roman officer of both the naval and land services, compiled an encyclopaedia in the first century AD. His hand written *Historia Naturalis* was one of the first books to be translated into English and printed. In it, Pliny describes how to "drive away the unclean dreams of venery" using the plant Porcellayn (*portulaca oleracea*). Contemporaneously, Dioscorides, another military surgeon, wrote *De Materia Medica*, which remained a medical textbook well into the seventeenth century. In it he also recommends Porcellayn to quench "the outrageous desire to lust" of the body.

Philosophy and the practice of medicine began to drift apart. Plato wrote of Hippocrates with respect as if he were a descendant of Asclepius; indeed, Hippocrates probably did study in Asclepius's temple at Cos in the 4th century BC but his approach to the treatment of disease was not through incubation. His *Hippocratic Collection* of medical procedures distinguished between medical or surgical treatment of disease on one hand and the philosophical and religious alternative approach on the other. Medicine became a science.

Hippocrates was followed by Galen who worked between 130 and 200 AD. His anatomical dissections convinced him that arteries were filled with blood rather than air as had been previously thought, and his work listing the properties of herbs was studied by physicians all over Europe. The herbals of the Middle Ages were based on his work with the additions of an ever increasing *materia medica*.

Artemidorus

The dream dictionary of Artemidorus has become the main basis for popular dream divination. Published from old manuscripts when printing was invented, it lingers on into the dream dictionaries of today.

Artemidorus, a Greek geographer and possibly an initiate of a sect of Apollo, lived in the first century before Christ when incubation was still the main diagnostic tool for health and prognostication. His maps of the world are lost but his *Oneirocritica*, a book of dream interpretations, survives. His work may be seen as the precursor to modern psychoanalysis which, stymied by religious dogma, was not allowed to progress until the last century.

Artemidorus insisted that, for the correct interpretation of a dream to be reached, the interpreter must be aware of life events leading up to the dream as well as the occupation and lifestyle of the dreamer. He was interested in whether the dream was connected with others or a single occurrence. In his time, life was simpler than it is today. It was easier for a dream diviner to understand the description of a dream. His patients lived in country villages or small towns where the lifestyle was very similar. Television, mass education, varied beliefs and holidays abroad were in the future. It was easier for the priest diviner to understand the inwardnesses of a dream once he were aware of the dreamer's family life, his hopes and fears, and the events leading up to the dream. Nowadays, so many occasions mean totally different things to analyst and dreamer that it is often impossible for a listener to understand exactly what picture his dreamer is trying to show him.

However, this scientific approach soon got forgotten and his dream dictionary has become the cornucopia of the amateur dream interpreter. Bees mean money; goats, bad news; birds mean a journey: these analyses may be fun over the breakfast table but have no universal authenticity. Take the last example where birds mean a journey. In the Middle East, swallows migrate at wintertime and any herdsman would be aware that their advent presaged a change in climate, perhaps necessitating a movement of his flock to other pastures. A dream of swallows in late autumn is quite likely for such a herdsman. He would be looking for them. We do not. In the northern hemisphere the Vs of migrating geese have little relevance while daily weather forecasts are omnipresent. So dreaming of birds probably has another, more personal, meaning that a dream dictionary cannot supply.

Greek mythology

Apollo, second only to Zeus, the father of the gods, was associated with prognostications and dreams. He was thought to be able to avert or inflict evil of all kinds. It was worth sacrificing an animal to be assured of his benevolence to your loved ones. His power to make your crops fruitful and your animals healthy required obeisance. Apollo's priests were mighty and their god so commanding that he became the main god of human well-being and the god of law. Their temples flourished from Rome to Asia Minor. The Pythia at the Temple of Apollo in Delphi, better known for her oracular utterances, was equally adept at incubation.

As years went on, a new god of medicine appeared called Asclepius. Mentioned by Homer as a physician whose sons were doctors in the Greek camp before the walls of Troy, Asclepius became deified as the son of Apollo.

The story goes that Zeus, jealous of his medical skills, killed him with a thunderbolt to prevent him making all men immortal. Asclepius was especially interested in incubation. His temple at Epidaurus was a well known resort for those in need of dream interpretation or who hoped that sleeping in the temple would cure their disease. Many stone tablets were discovered at Epidaurus listing these cures and dream interpretations, probably left by grateful customers. It appears from them that in that temple the sacrifice of a cock was the most usual offering following a successful treatment. This would not be beyond the means of most people of the time so Epidaurus would have been a popular hospital.

During these years dream analysis at a temple became a routine and apparently effective diagnostic procedure for disease or distress. Treatment might follow or not depending on the circumstances. Incubation was introduced to Rome in about 300 BC to cure a plague and the practice flourished there, only losing credence to Christianity.

Early Christian thoughts on dreams

In later years the Christian Church frowned on dreams as heresy. They were said to be the result of possession by an incubus or succubus, a male or female demon from Hell, who was trying to take over your mind as it lay unprotected in sleep. Sexual dreams had to be kept secret and, if possible, avoided.

St Ambrose composed a prayer to ward off night-time miasmas:

"Take away dreams and nightmares. Suppress that which

is foreign to us lest it defile our bodies."

Celibate clergy might be more prone to dreams of intercourse than those whose sexual desires were satisfied by a wife or husband.

It was acceptable for holy men to have visions and dream dreams, however. In the New Testament, Acts, Chapter 16, Paul dreamed that a man from Macedonia asked him for help. On waking he accepted that this was a real need and set off at once for that country to preach. Paul was clearly a man of immense intelligence and his daytime activities must have taken up his conscious mind, but at night I would suggest that his brain made him aware of a need that had perhaps escaped his daytime cognition. He was in no doubt about what his dream meant. His whole life was bent on preaching for his God so this dream simply showed him accurately where his next mission should be.

In the Christmas story according to St Matthew, the three wise men arrived in Jerusalem enquiring, "Where is he who has been born King of the Jews? For we have seen his star in the East and come to worship him."

Herod, at that time King of Palestine under the Romans, was at once alerted to trouble in his territory and, bringing the three wise men before him, begged to be told where they were bound for so he too could worship before this new infant king. Parting with expressions of good will on each side, the wise men went on down to Bethlehem where they found the baby Jesus and gave him gifts, but were clearly warned by their dreams not to return to Jerusalem. They went home another way, escaping confrontation with Herod. However they must have communicated enough of their disquiet to the parents of Jesus that Joseph dreamed a sufficiently alarming dream to make him pack his family up and remove to Egypt where he remained until Herod had died and was no longer a threat. The account does not detail the actual dreams, which is a pity, but Joseph's were obviously dreams of pursuit and fear, leaving the recipient only the job of deciding whom to fear and flee from. In both cases there was little choice and he made the right analysis.

These stories do show that at the time of Jesus there was still credence in dream divination. People acted on what their dreams showed them and looked at their dreams in a scientific way. The Christian Church accepted this, while beginning to clamp down on the interpretation of the ordinary man's dreams, and this may have had its origin in the natural shedding of previous religious dogma with all its trappings that a new church must pursue to make its own place.

Christian Europe

William Turner, Dean of Wells and physician to the Duke of Somerset, writing in 1551, advocates lettuce seed to subdue ''unclean dreams'' and ''the rage of venery''. Dreams had become something to suppress not interpret. Turner goes on to advise Nymphea (water lily) for ''wifeless gentlemen and husbandless gentlewomen against the unclean dreaming of venery and filthy pollutions'' (probably ''wet dreams'').

It was a big change from the open acceptance and interpretation of sex dreams in the time of the Pharaohs. Turner went on to suggest peony as a remedy ''against the strangling of the nightmare,'' and reports that Tragus, who lived a hundred years before, used Polypody or wall fern ''against grievous and heavy dreams''.

So in the Christian era the use of incubation for diagnosis and treatment of disease declined as herbal and surgical treatments became more popular. The humours (blood, yellow choler, black choler and phlegm) were now thought to influence mind and body. Dreams were discounted as prognostications; rather, they were thought to be a form of possession by evil spirits and therefore discouraged. People did not speak about them any more. A valuable form of diagnosis was lost and remained so until modern times.

It was not a sudden change. Temple-goers dwindled and, when earthquakes or disuse destroyed them, they were not rebuilt. The growth of Christianity and the Moslem faith with its own doctors overtook priest-led incubation. The Crusaders, rampaging through the Byzantine Empire and the Middle East like bovver-boys on a Bank Holiday weekend, further destroyed the temples and the settled way of living that first the Greeks and then the Roman Empire had produced. Priest-physicians fled.

The spread of Christianity throughout Europe relegated dreams to a whispered telling to a trusted confidant or, wiser still, kept to yourself. At best accepted as abnormal thoughts and at worst demonic possession, treatment tended to be exhaustive and very often fatal. To be burned at the stake because your dream was considered to denote a working relationship with Satan led, not surprisingly, to extreme reticence or, at best, an abridged communication by the normal punter.

So the new Christians risked having their dreams pronounced blasphemy. Later on in the Middle Ages, sexual dreams of intercourse with someone or some thing other than your own wife or husband could even be interpreted as temptation by the Devil. Your soul might be thought to be in danger of succumbing. You could be judged as being the victim of succubus or incubus and your fate would be burning to purification. The general public, therefore, played safe and trivialised their nightly adventures into superstitions with universal meanings for each subject. This way they were safe from the cleansing arm of their church.

Freud

It was not until Freud exploded his *Interpretation of Dreams* upon the world that people began looking seriously at dreams again. Throughout Europe in the late nineteenth century neurologists were experimenting on animals to try to isolate the role various parts of the brain play in sleep. At the same time, psychologists sought a physical cause and reason for dreams and from centre after centre new work poured out in the scientific journals. Hildebrant and Strumpell were aware that dream memories might come from childhood. Delboeuf went further, saying that any life experience leaves an unalterable trace on the memory which may be recalled. Maury postulated that dreams passed in a second. This was later disproved.

Into this maelstrom of scientific activity strode Sigmund Freud (1856-1939). Experimental neurologist and qualified physician, classical scholar, speaking and reading French and English as well as his native German, Freud was well placed to be heard. He made sense of the current morass of knowledge and produced theories of dreaming and dream analysis, which, if they have not fully stood the passage of time, have set later workers well on the road. Founding the speciality of psychoanalysis to explore neurotic tendencies brought him fame and a lucrative livelihood which has been followed by many. Like all great scientists, he was aware of the limitations attending his theory of dream interpretation; namely that any bit of dream content may have a different meaning, depending on who dreamed it and what context it occurred in. Therefore his book *The Interpretation of Dreams* (published in 1900) mostly contains his own dreams as examples. He knew, as did Artemidorus, that he was the person best equipped to explain the significance of his own dreams. He postulated that you have a great well of memory built from infancy. As you grow, the more immediate memories suppress those from long ago. This store of normally unavailable memory he called your *unconscious*. Dreams, he felt, were powered by wishes. These might be everyday desires that you were well aware of. You would not dream of them, however, unless they were reinforced by the same wish deep in your unconscious.

He saw in the unconscious a mass of wishes and desires trying to get out but needing a hook from a recent day time experience to allow them through the censor mechanism that he believed imprisoned this powerful unconscious undercurrent of desires, built and trapped from infancy.

He suggested that your censor mechanism, which was in fact your social conscience, repressed your infantile, instinctual, uncontrolled desires so that you might grow up a normal, conforming member of society. He was aware too that the immediate feelings of your body could work their way into your dreams.

See Chapter 3 for more about Freud's theories.

Jung

Following him, Carl Gustav Jung, (1875-1961), a Swiss psychologist and psychiatrist went further, believing that the material held in your unconscious must be brought to mind and understood before its effect on your psychological state could be alleviated. This he called Analytical Psychology. He classified people into introverted or extroverted types, what we nowadays talk of as A-types (active pushy non-stop workers) and B-types (passive thinkers who are not so likely to put their blood pressures up). He said that, in everyone, one of the sensations (thinking, feeling, perception or intuition) predominates to make us what we are. He took issue with Freud on the sexual origin of psychoneuroses, suggesting that immediate problems and conflicts were a more likely cause than childhood hang-ups. He suggested that the will to live was Man's primary force, not sex, and in any analysis you had to take into account both the personal lifestyle of the patient as well as the behavioural patterns handed down to him by his ancestors. He felt that the body and mind were always trying to remain in equilibrium and dreams were part of that attempt, showing up irregularities in lifestyle.

Adler

Alfred Adler (1870-1937), an Austrian psychiatrist, again repudiated Freud's theory that sexual feelings, more or less repressed and often from childhood, were most people's motivation. He felt you were always trying to achieve a superiority of feeling and function within your society from an original feeling of inferiority. He found dream reports and childhood memories particularly useful in determining a patient's goals within his community.

21st Century dream analysis

These contending schools of thought, to name but a few, built an industry. Instrumentation, encouraged by Berger's invention of the encephalograph, allowed neurologists to plot the stages of sleep and allowed medical techniques to show that sleep and dreaming were triggered by chemical and hormonal substances reacting on centres deep in the brain.

This work continues and year by year scientists know more about the origin of and reason for dreaming. Psychoanalysts still use dream reports to highlight problems but normal people dream too. Your dreams, while perhaps not showing psychiatric problems, do show up the things that trouble you, and as such are useful in the everyday self-assessment of your feelings and motivations. There is now enough evidence of how to assess dreams to let you get to grips with a great deal of what your dreams are trying to tell you.

2

NORMAL SLEEP PATTERN AND NON-REM DREAMS

When do you dream?

You may believe that dreams only occur just before you wake. This is not so. Scientists have proved otherwise. They wake volunteers from all stages of sleep and have dreams reported.

How do they do this? In sleep laboratories, which are in effect little rooms with a comfortable bed, a volunteer sleeps with electrodes attached to his or her scalp to record brain activity through the night. After a night or two, most volunteers achieve sleep patterns that are normal for them, unlike the incubation sessions at a temple hundreds of years ago when stress dreams would have been more likely. At first, these tracings from the electrodes were inscribed on long rolls of paper throughout the night, but computerisation has cut this to a more simple form where each sleep stage is graphed to give an easily assessed reading. The mechanism is still just an updated version of the electroencephalograph apparatus invented by Berger that showed the world that sleep is not oblivion, but a time when your brain is active in a different way from that when you are awake.

The stages of sleep

When you shut your eyes, the electrical activity in your brain changes. The electroencephalograph shows a low irregular wave pattern. You are said to be entering Stage 1 non-Rapid Eye Movement (non-REM) sleep, and you feel the dropping off sensation that boring lectures or watching a late night television movie engender. This is close to the brain activity stage that those practising Transcendental Meditation reach. As your sleep deepens, small spindles of mounting waves and K complexes (where there is a sudden wave surge) creep into the wave pattern. When these are established you are in Stage 2 non-REM sleep. You can still wake easily from this stage if, for instance, someone calls your name or there is an unexpected sound. In fact, sounds are magnified to your sleeping ears in this stage. A cough sounds like gunfire, a knock on the door like a drum beat.

As you fall more deeply asleep and become less easily roused, your brain waves become large and slow and you are said to be passing through Stage 3 into Stage 4 non-REM sleep. At this point you are fast asleep and not easily roused. It is in these deep stages of non-REM sleep that growth hormone is released into your bloodstream. This hormone furthers the growth of children and masterminds the repair of damaged tissue in the fully-grown adult.

As the night progresses you tend to move back into the lighter stages of sleep and then into REM sleep (also called paradoxical sleep), where the brain waves become irregular, low and spiky.

The circulation to your brain is greatly increased in REM sleep, a sign of enhanced activity, and it appears to be a time when your brain is looking after itself and preparing for the day ahead. It is in REM sleep that you mostly experience dreams. This appears to be the make and mend time for your brain. New born babies slip in and out of REM sleep for the first three months, after which their sleep pattern becomes much more like that of an adult. This makes sense when you realise that babies are usually born with a complete physical form but their nervous system is still not fully developed and over the first three months catches up with their physical maturity.

The Babinski reflex, where tickling the sole of a baby's foot elicits big toe movement, is a standard check of how baby's nervous system is maturing. At birth the movement is upward, similar to that in an adult who has had a stroke involving the brain motor area and paralysing that leg. At three months the Babinski reflex shows a downward curl of the big toe which is the normal reflex in an adult.

Towards morning REM sleep stages alternate with gradually lightening stages of non-REM sleep, where the hormones prolactin and cortisol are released into the bloodstream as a sort of 'wake-up' jolt to your system.

The body's cycle

Doctors know that you have a sleep/wake cycle, called the 'circadian rhythm', which acts throughout the full twenty-four hours of a day to control your temperature and sleep pattern, so that your temperature drops slightly in the afternoon and in the evening, accompanied by a need for sleep at these times. In temperate regions we often ignore the afternoon blip and work through it, but a siesta is a common habit in many countries and one encouraged by the circadian body rhythm.

Through the day, especially if you are concentrating on a job, you find that about every one and a half to two hours you feel you need to take a breather, stretch and maybe have something to eat or drink, and then go back to whatever you were doing. This pattern is governed by an inbuilt daily clock deep in your midbrain that keeps this ultradian rhythm running through the day. It was not until the invention of the encephalograph that doctors were able to show that this rhythm also continued through the night, moving you through each stage of sleep with about 90 to 120 minutes in each stage. The usual pattern is to move quite quickly into deep sleep, then into lighter stages, perhaps returning to deep sleep and then lighter again, before going into REM sleep for a while, and then returning to the lighter stages of non-REM sleep and REM sleep until you wake in the morning.

The physical activity in sleep

In REM sleep, nervous command of your muscles is switched off. All the muscles of the body lie flaccid and unmoving, except for that great bellows of a muscle, the diaphragm, which continues to supply your power to breathe, and the small muscles around the eye which contract in an uncontrolled way, causing the eyes to move behind their lids. Look at a baby sleeping and you will see that movement which, in fact, gives the name to this part of sleep. The muscle paralysis is a safety feature. You cannot follow out the wild happenings in your dreams. You are pinioned to your bed although you dream of leaping from the window sill and flying through the air. In some very rare disturbances of sleep this paralysis fails and the effects may be catastrophic. Doctors seek then to restore normal lack of 'muscle function' and to suppress REM sleep until they do.

Because of the flaccidity of the muscles in REM sleep, especially the normal ancillary muscles of breathing (between the ribs, the musculature of soft palate and around the throat) it is in this phase of sleep that breathing problems such as the snoring of a blocked upper throat and sleep apnoeic episodes tend to start. There may also be a connection with some forms of cot death, which is more common in the first few months of life. Later, REM sleep does not form such a large proportion of the normal sleep pattern.

Sleep paralysis

Sometimes, usually following a noise or disturbance, you wake so suddenly that the normal recovery of movement has not quite occurred. You feel imprisoned in a dream, helpless and unprotected as you strive to move. Suddenly you are free. It is as if you are suddenly hit by movement. People used to think that their soul left their bodies in sleep to wander about the world. These wanderings were half remembered in dreams. The returning soul could be felt as a jolt as it re-entered your body, enlivening it again. This is not so. It is merely the switch back to normal enervation of the muscles that is felt. If you know that, you have no need to panic when you wake suddenly in REM sleep and find your arms and legs won't move. Don't fight it. Relax. In a second or less, movement returns to your limbs without a struggle.

Dreaming through the night

Woken in a sleep laboratory from any of the stages of sleep, volunteers report dreams to the scientists who wake them. Not so many dreams are reported after being roused from non-REM sleep as are reported following REM sleep and the non-REM dreams are usually less bizarre. However, it is by doing this that scientists came to accept that dreams occur in all parts of sleep, but because you do not wake at that time you do not remember them. The dream episode is washed away by further sleep, without you having any time awake to reinforce the images in your mind and so lay them down in your memory.

You are most likely to remember the dreams experienced during the second half of the night in REM sleep. They are the most easily remembered, probably because you wake from them with a mind already becoming active for the next day. Waking in the middle of the night, you are motivated to minimise thought so that sleep may return. Unless your dream is bizarre enough to remain with you until you wake again, or unless you jot down the main features to remind yourself when you wake in the morning, you may know that you dreamed but not remember any more than that.

Forgotten dreams

Dreams are ephemeral things, extraordinarily so. It is hard to understand why such incredible happenings can be forgotten so easily. From long ago this has puzzled philosophers and scientists. Is it that dreams have no continuity? Is it that they are illogical adventures? Do they leap from scene to scene with no regard for time or distance or likelihood?

Some sleep psychologists believe that all things you experience go into your short term memory and, from there, if they remain with you for a few minutes, begin to be laid down in your long term memory bank. From there, they may be retrieved either at will or by another memory that leads into that particular part of your memory store.

Dreams early in the night are washed off your short term memory by your continuing sleep, or may be laid down where you can no longer retrieve them. However, if you wake right after a dream, even early in the night, and take the time to write it down or lie there going over it in your mind so that it has time to be stored in the longer term memory banks, you have much more chance of remembering it next morning.

This dream evanescence is not peculiar to your night-time brain function, but it is irritatingly obvious then. By day, being introduced to a line of people leaves you without any but the last couple of names, unless you are trained in fast memory work, and can shift the list of names from your short term memory into longer term storage.

Good public relations executives repeat each name out loud and try to fix some trigger memory beside the name. They look for oddities of face or dress or manner to file against the new name and they concentrate on each new introduction for long enough to allow the transition from short term to long term memory to begin.

The fact that your dreams are often totally unconnected increases the difficulty of recall.

I believe that your brain does not need you to remember most dreams because they are just the routine organisation that your brain works away at during your sleep time to attain peace of mind and allow you to have an unworried day. It is only when this routine organisation breaks down (because your brain cannot sort out a particular emotion or problem) that it dresses it up in weird pictures and presents it to your waking mind. These dreams are so strong in content that they not only wake you but also allow you to remember them.

People in the sleep laboratory who are wakened when they are in various stages of sleep and asked to recall what they were dreaming often report rather banal and unexciting dreams. These are easily forgotten. I believe they are not meant to be remembered. To make an analogy, you are getting a look in at the smoothly working office that is your brain at night. It is sorting out the memories and feelings of the day, throwing out old thoughts that you don't need and placing others in store. It does not need the daytime brain mechanisms to interfere. How your brain stores memories is still unknown but it is clear that it is not alphabetic as we do filing in the office. The office of the brain works differently. From my experience I see in my mind a sort of huge old-fashioned telephone exchange where the enormous area supplied by the convoluted cortex of the brain is used as a storage unit.

Memory triggers

I think that memories are stored in chronological order, as well as by importance to you. There may be no actual link between stored memories but it does appear that if one memory is triggered others come up with it; sometimes memories that you had thought you had forgotten or had not come to you for years. That happens often enough in your waking brain but more so in your dreaming brain because if something is being slotted in to a certain place the memories round it are also disturbed.

The enormous increase in blood supply with its increase in nutrients and oxygen circulating through the brain in dream sleep facilitates this greater mobilisation of memory material because the purpose of that part of sleep is memory re-setting and storage. It may even assist with memory retrieval. Who has not gone to sleep worrying because they could not remember a name or a place from long ago only to find it easily available the next morning?

Because there seems to be a time lag in the storage system, in that you do dream of things that happen to you the day before you sleep and then not so often until after three to five days have passed, it is possible to see what memories are thrown up by talking about some long ago memory that was powerful at the time.

Remembered dreams

Sometimes your daytime desires or agonies of mind are so strong that attaining peace of mind for the next day is impossible. The emotion will not tolerate being slotted into any memory bank. The night-time brain mechanism then says, "O.K. I can't lay this memory away or mitigate it so that you reach peace of mind by morning. I am going to present it as a wildly coloured picture that your waking brain will remember and through the day you will have to sort out the emotion and gain some acceptance of it or the same sort of vivid, upsetting dream will occur on the next night." These are the dreams you remember and these are the dreams you experience in REM sleep.

Sleep onset dreams

Outside the laboratory, you are not usually aware of the dreams you have at sleep onset or the ones that are reported from being woken in deep non-REM sleep. However, if you are woken by the phone or some other noise, either during deep sleep or just after you have dropped off, you will realise that you have been dreaming and you could reinforce that dream in your mind by going over it or writing it down to be looked at the next morning.

So, before you forget these non-REM dreams as being unlikely occurrences (and get on with working out the meanings of the REM dreams that provide most of your night-time adventures), let us look at them.

Sleep onset dreams are little use for analysis as they do not have the same causation as REM dreams. Unless you wake just after falling asleep you won't know you are having them. They are not trying to highlight some sort of psychological problem that you have to solve. They are part of your passage into the deeper stages of non-REM sleep.

When you go to bed your thoughts are under your control. You may daydream a bit about the "might have been", or tell yourself a story, or just go over the happenings of the day. Gradually, however, your thinking slows. The fantasies and waking dreams slide on into a stage where you are not aware that you have left reality behind. You are no longer orientated in time or space. You do not know where you are and cannot control your thoughts which become more and more bizarre, gradually allowing you to enter deep non-REM sleep.

These are not daydreams under your control. Wake after nodding off and see how far away from reality your thoughts have led you. These dreams are usually visual hallucinations, as you may feel you are touching an object that is not there. You may even wake thinking a familiar voice has called you, leaving you to wonder if this is some sort of extra-sensory perception. I have never found it to be so. Interestingly, taste and smell sensations seldom enter these sleep onset dreams.

The difference between sleep onset dreams and REM dreams

These fantasies are, however, true dreams and are part of what your brain is working on during this period of your sleep. Sleep onset dreams are unlike REM dreams in that they come from daydreams, which are under the waking control of your mind. They arise from your daytime thoughts and considerations. REM dreams do not. REM dreams are thought to be associated with unconscious wishes and fears within your mind as well as being influenced by external and internal stimuli (see Chapter 7). You are unlikely to begin a REM dream from an extension of your waking thoughts, though material from day time occurrences may well find a place in your REM dream.

REM dreams are usually associated with physical signs of sexual arousal and sleep onset dreams are not. In fact, if a man complains that he is unable to achieve an erection it is possible to check whether his problem stems from physical or psychological causes by allowing him to sleep in a sleep laboratory and, when the sleeping trace from his brain shows that he is in REM stage sleep, checking to see whether he has an erection or not. Repeated lack of erection during REM sleep would tend to support a diagnosis of a physical cause, whereas finding an erection in REM sleep allows the doctor to reassure his patient and treat the condition as an emotional problem.

The significance of sleep onset dreams

These dreams can be a pointer to you about the sort of personality you have, and as such can be used to indicate your general state of mind. Sleep onset dreams appear to be more common to people of a self-accepting type. Rigid, conforming, intolerant people have them less frequently. If you tend towards narrow-mindedness you seem less able to let your mind go wandering than those people who are more laid back and socially secure. It is not a failure in your personality; it is just the way you are. You tend to crash straight into sleep or lie awake and worry until sleep claims you. You can't let your mind take you wandering thought by thought into a waking dream as does someone who is perhaps more securely poised within their social environment.

Sleep onset dreamers' dreams reflect their ability to let go. Their daydreams may lead them into sleep comfortably, though in some cases it may take them longer to "get over" than it does the more uptight personality who simply crashes out.

Sleep onset dreaming may not be useful for interpretation, but may be used for self-assessment. If you have never been able to day dream and realise you have become a highly strung rigid personality you may want to try to become more relaxed and easy going by using mental and physical relaxation techniques such as the Alexander Technique, Yoga exercises or meditation.

However, if you put your head on the pillow and crash out, this is just as good a way into sleep. There is no special benefit in having sleep onset dreams. They merely appear to be associated with laid back, socially confident types who are not ruled by conventions.

Inspirational dreams

It does sometimes happen that your waking dreams allow leaps of conjecture that can provide the answers to problems that you have been mulling over. There is a story about Frederich August Kekule, the renowned German chemist, who was sitting half asleep by his fireside, wondering for the umpteenth time how to explain the chemical formula of benzene when there appeared to be too few carbon atoms to make up the usual straight chain model of a molecule. As he dozed off, his thoughts became fantastic, as they do in sleep onset dreams, and he saw the lines of atoms wriggling about like snakes. Suddenly one of them caught hold of its own tail and started to whirl around. Kekule woke to this picture and realised that he had just seen in this ring the rationalisation of the benzene molecule.

So, faced with an insoluble problem, if struggling with it and tearing your mind to pieces does not bring a solution, it might be a good idea for you to relax and let your mind run free. See if sleep onset dreaming can bring alternative resolutions to your mind.

Lateral thinking is very much a product of sleep onset dreaming. Use it to enhance your imagination. If you have an amazing idea as you nod off, you usually wake with it so you need not fear having it washed away by the advancing tide of sleep. It is wise, however, to write it down before you venture into sleep again.

Falling dreams

A sudden feeling of falling that brings you awake is quite common in the early stages of sleep. It is probably instigated by a sudden noise or internal stimulus, such as a muscle twitch, which shocks you out of Stage 1 or 2 non-REM sleep. All your muscles contract in the same way that a baby's do in the Moro reflex, a primitive reflex causing an infant to appear to grab forward as if onto a parental figure, as baby monkeys do when afraid. You may remember a short dream leading up to it like pushing a wheelbarrow over a cliff or tripping on a step, or you may not remember a dream at all. Although common, it has no apparent significance. If it happens often it is sensible to check that your bedroom is quiet enough for sound sleep to develop. It may also occur if you are in an excitable state about something when your gentle passage into sleep may be disturbed by sudden distress or excitement.

Lucid dreams

Just occasionally in a dream you are aware that you are dreaming. Usually you are close to waking when this happens. You are in some unusual place doing something odd and you say to yourself, ''This is just a dream and I will wake soon.''

This sort of awareness is called 'Lucid Dreaming'.

Some people think it is a gift that should be encouraged. They feel, as many analysts feel, that dreams are a path into your unconscious store of memories and, if you could train yourself to enter that store knowingly, you would be able to browse around like you do at a library, picking up a memory here and there and using your cerebral store more effectively.

I do not think this is so. Encouraging yourself to be able to reach a state where you are aware that you are dreaming so that you can influence what happens in that dream is counter-productive.

Dreams tell you what your unconscious is struggling with. To change that, changes the message your dreaming brain is trying to give you. It defeats the purpose of the dream, which is to point you to the problems that prevent your peace of mind. You are meant to remember the dream and act on it. Change the dream and you lose that message.

What you are likely to be doing in lucid dreaming is rising into a sort of mixture of REM and light non-REM sleep stages, where you have partial control over your thoughts. This sort of dreaming can be used to nullify nightmares and is close to one of my techniques for doing so, although I do not think you need to enter REM sleep to find a pleasant finish to a nightmare. You know that a nightmare stems from over-whelming anxiety. Ameliorating its ending is beneficial. You can then avoid repetition of its horror. You are also well aware that you must disperse your anxiety during the day to prevent nightmare repetition. Lucid dreaming, if you can achieve it may be also used for this purpose. Few actually manage it to any degree.

In addition, to encourage yourself to move into the lighter stages of REM and non-REM sleep as soon as you start to dream is counter productive. You will not only shorten the length of time when your brain is sorting your memory functions, you will also miss those messages with strong feelings attached that your brain is trying to get across to you.

Deep sleep dreaming

Dreaming in the deeper stages of sleep appears to be mostly banal. You seldom wake suddenly from deep sleep, night terrors being perhaps the only exception. It is only in the laboratory that volunteers are shaken from their slumbers to report any dreams they are having. If you are woken you usually feel so muddled and disorientated that any dream is rapidly forgotten.

Physical benefits of deep sleep

The Indian religious texts known as the Upanishads say that in deep sleep you are close to your real self. You desire nothing, dream nothing but are close to mortality and Brahma. This may be spiritually acceptable, but in fact in deep non-REM sleep the body is looking after itself. Growth hormone is released into the bloodstream to circulate through the tissues to promote repair and encourage growth in children. Who has not been thankful to slip into the deep dreamless healing sleep that comes towards the end of any acute infection and wake feeling enormously better?

Night terrors

Night terrors are particular to deep non-REM sleep. Night terrors are not nightmares. They occur in deep Stage 3 and 4 non-REM sleep, whereas nightmares are anxiety dreams and are found in REM sleep. Night terrors are not uncommon in children. They are a frightening experience for any parent. If you happen to be watching, you will see your child sit up in bed suddenly, often with his eyes wide open. He then starts to scream and throw himself about. Gathering him to you and comforting him has no effect. You cannot reach his senses. He is, in fact, deeply asleep locked in with whatever horror is motivating his reaction. He sweats. His heartbeat leaps to a fantastic rate and just when you, his parents, are at your wits' end your child lies back and continues to sleep as if nothing had happened. Even if you manage to waken him, he will just turn over and go back into quiet sleep. Usually children have no recollection of the episode next morning and do not report any extraordinary dreams.

Children usually grow out of night terrors, just as they outgrow sleepwalking, which occurs in the same part of non-REM sleep. They are rare even in children and there is often a familial tendency. Boys are more usually affected than girls.

Night terrors occur within the first three hours of going to sleep when most deep sleep occurs. They are extremely rare in adult life, a good thing because the sight of a fully-grown man screaming and throwing himself about in the middle of the night is a frightening and uncontrollable experience. An adult with night terrors certainly needs urgent professional help because adults are too big to control easily and so may hurt themselves or others in the throes of a terror.

Treatment of night terrors

Make sure your child is all right and does not hurt himself during the time of throwing himself about. Offer reassurance and, if you feel it appropriate, gentle encouragement to waken. See that he does not hurt himself, and wait. Your child will either wake and just go back to sleep again as if nothing has happened or he will return to quiet sleep without waking. In the morning you, his parents, may be shattered but he will not remember anything about it. There is usually little doubt when a child is having a night terror and a sleep specialist may be able to facilitate the investigation and amelioration of any pent up feelings of aggression or distress, as well as to exclude other night-time problems such as fits, which may give a slightly similar picture. Night terrors are very frightening episodes for parents to cope with and unless very mild and infrequent should, I believe, be reported to your doctor.

People with night terrors in sleep laboratories are wakened fully and some report sudden and terrible feelings of being choked or shut in small spaces. Susceptible people may trigger a night terror by hearing a certain sound or have it triggered by some physical stimulus. Unexpressed aggression and fear may also be the basis of night terrors, so if your child has night terrors, try to find out during the day, if he has any secret fears or anger bottled up. Is he being bullied at school? Is he being expected to perform better than he is able? Is he anxious about the stability of his home life? It is amazing what makes children anxious, as so often they keep their worries to themselves. As the child does not remember having a night terror he is not going to volunteer the memory of a bad dream. It is up to his parents to elicit any hidden anxieties and have them laid to rest.

There are medicines that can suppress Stage 4 non-REM sleep and so halt the occurrence of night terrors in the short term. When these are stopped the terrors just seem to recur unless the cause has been found and the feeling of aggression allayed. Children need Stage 4 sleep because that is the main time when the growth hormone is secreted, but adults also require this hormone to facilitate healing and tissue regrowth so long term treatment that prevents Stage 4 sleep is not an option.

Sleepwalking

Sleepwalking also occurs during the deep stages of non-REM sleep and this too tends to run in families and be confined to childhood. There is no definitive causation known for sleepwalking. Some doctors suggest that in children the cause may be physiological because it tends to occur in early childhood and be banished by the physiological changes that puberty brings. They suggest that sleepwalking occurring in adulthood is less likely to disappear by itself, and that psychological causes (as well as alcohol overuse and other substance abuse) may be causative factors.

Sleepwalkers do not give the picture of confused wandering that demented patients show. Their movements are more purposeful. Children often get up from bed, go to the bathroom, urinate and go back to bed while still deeply asleep. They may only be found to be asleep if their parents try to talk to them or if they miss their way and choose the wrong room. They may move their toys about or appear to play with them and then go back to bed. They may just sit up in bed for a few minutes and then lie back down. If wakened gently or just encouraged they will return to bed and sleep and have forgotten all about it in the morning.

Stress, tiredness or fever are all said to encourage sleepwalking so if your children do it, make sure they are not worried about anything, and that they are not overtired or unwell. There is a strong family tendency so if your family have a history of sleepwalking it is sensible to be aware that your children might also sleepwalk.

In some rare adult cases, obstructive sleep apnoea (heavy snorers whose oxygen supply is attenuated in sleep) and some medicines may be the cause. Treatment of the condition or stopping the medication may then be curative.

If you sleepwalk or have sleepwalkers in your family it is important to make sure that you and they remain safe during the episodes. Unguarded stairs, open doors and widely opening windows should not be accessible. Passageways should be kept clear and if the walker has a definite pattern he or she should have a lighted path so that gentle wakening may be encouraged into familiar surroundings. This may be especially important if a sleepwalker is away from home in unfamiliar surroundings, for instance in a hotel. It is a myth that sleepwalkers never come to harm. Again this is a condition that should be discussed with your doctor.

Sleep talking

Sleep talking is not associated with night terrors or sleepwalking and is much more common. It occurs in all stages of sleep and may be clear and decisive or just mumbles. It is possible to have conversations with sleep talkers where they do seem to be answering your questions although you get the feeling that it is merely the sound of a voice stimulating speech in the sleeper and not an accurate answer. Sleep talkers do not give away secrets for the asking. It is unlikely that the speaker and the sleeper are both on the same subject. It appears to be caused by stimulation of the speech centre in the brain and may be associated with dreaming.

Like sleepwalking and sleep terrors, stress may encourage sleep talking and to that extent may be a sign to you that you need to unwind more, relax in mind and body and look for peace of mind.

3

FREUD'S THEORIES ON DREAMING

It is hard to write a book on dreams without taking a look at what Freud did to bring dream interpretation back into medicine as a diagnostic tool of psychiatric problems. More extreme ideas are ascribed to him than he did actually suggest and it is perhaps worth spending a little time considering his actual theories. Psychoanalysts may no longer subscribe to his rather authoritarian beliefs, but they give credit where it is due and accept that he was the father of their speciality. He made dream analysis a medical subject again after six hundred years of neglect and suspicion.

Freud suggested that dreams arose from thoughts engendered by your beliefs and the type of personality you have. He also knew that dreams could arise from physical stimuli, both intrinsic and from the everyday world you see around you. These tenets have not changed but it would be unrealistic to think that one middle class, middle aged, middle European man, with few laboratory results to go on would get it all right.

The Id, Ego and Super Ego

He suggested that as you grow up you hide your uncontrolled and aggressive desires behind a wall of learned self-control, allowing you to operate as the socially integrated personality you become as an adult. This well of hidden desire he called your 'unconscious' and, later, your Id. The wall or censor mechanism which suppresses your desires he named your Super Ego, and your everyday self he called your Ego.

The unconscious

He saw the unconscious as a huge morass of all the untamed desires from your babyhood. He felt that children were born with strong sexual urges and aggressive desires for food and achievement. Society and education dictate that you bury these as you grow up, in order to live at peace and in happiness with your neighbours.

However, like an unstable volcanic core, the unconscious is always ready to burst out. In sleep, your Super Ego could become less rigid, allowing these buried desires to leap in to your consciousness in dreams. To do this, Freud suggested, they needed a strong daytime thought or desire that could reach in through the weakened night-time Super Ego and pick up a similar buried wish, manifesting it in your dreams.

Parental desires

He believed that, because in babyhood your nearest objects of desire are your parents, you must desire either your mother or your father sexually, as well as wanting their presence to provide food and comfort. This then suggested to him that you must, therefore, hate the other parent and wish to usurp his or her place in all things.

He wrote that, in his experience, the chief predisposing factor in all those children who later became neurotic were their unresolved relationships with their parents. He suggested that, as normal babies grow up, these strong primal desires change. Their world grows wider and takes in other people with whom they make relationships of love, respect and even dislike. They cease to see their parents as their whole world. In fact, by the time they are walking, they have a host of other people to interact with and in the most natural way become less dependent on their parents. In adolescence, they go to the other extreme, shrugging off the last protective parental apron strings and striking out on their own in thought and action. They are then readying themselves for the responsibility of caring relationships of their own where they make their own family circle. At this time, Freud thought, your own unconscious urges are mirrored by your Ego and transferred to someone of your own choice. (Who has not heard the phrase at a wedding, ''He's married his mother''?)

Neuroses

However, in cases where this natural psychological maturity does not take place, or is warped by circumstances, children might fail to reach this equilibrium in adulthood. These cases of non-maturation were the patients Freud saw and wrote about. They had neuroses which he felt were caused by their inability to grow up mentally, in the natural fashion. Although by day they could subdue their desires behind the screen of their Super Ego, their emotional designs upon their parents could become envisaged by night in their dreams when the weakened Super Ego allowed their horrible thoughts through into consciousness. He used their dreams to show him where their failure to achieve a normal adulthood started and then tried to put this right.

Dreams as a reflection of the unconscious

Freud was convinced that, without a similar wish in the conscious, no one could retrieve the greater wish warping the unconscious. Like many experts, he was willing to bend facts to support his case and so his wish-fulfilment theories have become discounted. His writings do still have something to tell us about dream classification, and these he worked out from his acute observation of his patients without modern encephalographs or animal experimentation: a quite exceptional effort.

One young woman he treated came to him following a period when she had begun to show extreme aversion to her mother, hitting her and shouting to her to stay away. At the same time she had been perfectly content to be friends with her much older sister. Freud saw her when, although her overt hostility had ceased, she had begun to have her sleep disturbed by troublesome dreams where she was at funerals for an older woman or was sitting at a table with her sister with both of them in black mourning clothes.

Freud felt she had managed to push her hate of her mother into her unconscious where it could only return in dreams, but was nonetheless there and powerfully affecting her general behaviour because coupled with the dreams, which were clearly a wish fulfilment of her mother's death, she also had an obsessive anxiety as to the lady's well being, constantly having to rush home to make sure she was still alive. He goes on to propound the theory that a hysterical girl who seems obsessively fond of her mother is so for a similar reason. She secretly wishes her mother dead, pushes the unacceptable feeling into her subconscious where it can only show in dreams, but, because the thought is a powerful one, it has an effect on her behaviour, leaving her over-anxious about her mother.

Modern scepticism about Freud's theories

In a way this is such an obnoxious theory that it hastened the end of Freud's supremacy. Normal people did not want to be made to feel that they hated their parents and secretly sought to supplant them in their other parent's affections. It has that grain of truth that sticks in your craw. In the animal kingdom it occurs naturally and without censure. The old lioness yields place to her daughters and the old lion first throws his adult sons from the pride and then in his turn is chased from his position of supremacy into obscurity or death by a younger, stronger rival. Modern educated Man has moved so far from the animal model that any love/hate of your parents becomes, in my opinion, a residual and unimportant factor in your widening experience of life. Freud, after all, was seeing neurotic patients with serious hang-ups whose previous life-style was probably abnormal. It is interesting that he too stresses the necessity of the analyst being aware of his patient's background and family situation and he asked his patients to tell him what they thought their dreams meant and discussed that feeling in depth.

The Oedipus Complex

Freud's theory had its basis in his wide classical education, which was the norm for middle class children of his time. The stories of Greek heroes and heroines and their tangled relationships appeared a rational foundation for all relationships and he certainly named neurotic complexes with Greek names. The Oedipus Complex was one such. Sophocles's play, *Oedipus Rex*, was well known to Freud. He saw in its gradual unwinding of the facts the human condition that led to neurotic behaviour.

The story goes that Oedipus was the son of Jocasta and King Laius of Thebes. They left him in the wilderness to die as soon as he was born because an Oracle had warned Laius that this child would kill him. However, the baby was rescued, adopted by the King and Queen of another country and brought up as their son. When he was grown up he also consulted the Oracle, as was the custom of the time. Horrified to learn that his fate was to kill his father and marry his mother, he left the court he had been brought up in at once so that the prediction could not come true. Unfortunately, on his travels he met his natural father, Laius, quarrelled with him and, in the ensuing fight, killed him, unaware that he was his son.

Going on to Thebes, he solved the riddle that the Sphinx set to all who wished to enter the city. In gratitude the Thebans made him their King and gave him Jocasta's hand in marriage. Oedipus ruled Thebes well for many years and, happy in his marriage, had two sons and two daughters with Jocasta. Then a plague broke out and the Thebans went once more to their Oracle, asking how to get rid of the infection. The Oracle told them that only when Laius's murderer had been driven from the land would the plague cease to trouble them. When eventually Oedipus realised what he had done he was so horrified that he blinded himself and went into exile.

Freud's interpretation of the Oedipus story

Freud felt that his neurotic patients, similarly unaware of repressed sexual desires for one or other parent coupled with hate for the other, mortified themselves into an abnormal and unhappy lifestyle. He said that they had buried their unworthy desires so deeply that they were no longer aware of them and only in sleep could these anti-social wishes be brought to the surface. He and his patient could then discuss the problem and allow his patient to discard the enormous feelings of guilt, as he or she understood that these emotions were normal for children and thereafter merely had to be sublimated into other acceptable loving relationships within society.

Using Freud's ideas

This theory in its entirety tells us much about the mores of the rather rigid society that Freud lived in and perhaps even more about his own thoughts and feelings. Rubbishing Freud is easy because, like many experts who propound a certain theory, he insisted on finding a love/hate parental relationship as the cause of *all* the neuroses he saw. Later psychologists and psychoanalysts founded their own rigid theories, but as experimental and physiological findings become available it is clear that no one theory fits every case.

Where Freud cannot be faulted is in his insistence that a cured neurotic patient was at peace with himself. Whether or not you have a deep sexual or physical need for one or other parent in babyhood, he is certainly correct in suggesting that as you grow up you widen your circle of acquaintance and gradually lose your dependence on your parents, becoming your own person with loves and hates for other people and things. He is also correct in thinking that dreams have meaning and he was aware that the dreamer himself or herself was best placed to discover what the dream suggested.

Interestingly, in Sophocles's play Jocasta dismisses Oedipus's telling of his dream that he had lain with his mother and had sex with her as commonplace. She says that most men have dreamed such a dream and just disregarded it. Sophocles wrote in about 400 BC when dreams were clearly discussed at every level and dream content was not a forbidden subject. I shall be discussing sexual dreams and their meaning in a later chapter. Just now, it is sufficient to accept that people owe Freud some respect for bringing dreams back into general interest. Without him dreams might still be taboo.

4

REM DREAMS

Dreams that you experience in REM sleep are useful in getting a picture of your state of mind. These are the dreams that psychologists and psychoanalysts from Freud onwards hoped would become the ''high road'' leading to your unconscious thoughts.

There are many theories of dream causation and about whether they are purely casual mind pictures or even predestination. Reading about these theories leads you inevitably to the feeling that dreams do have some part in the process of quietening your mind. Your brain constantly seeks equilibrium of mood, and dreams have a function in helping you to reach this state.

The 'central core'

One of the more attractive theories suggests that dreams are the product of a central core of energy in your brain that is particularly yours and is the origin of your personality. It is a sort of inbuilt engine of self-stimulation, if you like to look at it that way, the get-up-and-go that is particularly yours and makes you the type of person you are. When this central source of energy is working hard, the blood circulation to your brain is greatly increased to allow a plentiful source of oxygen and nutritive substance to flood the working area, as well as to facilitate the removal of waste products. Rapid Eye Movement sleep occurs at one of these times and some modern theorists suggest that, as your core self-stimulation increases, dreams are formed.

Why are dreams formed?

Perhaps because your brain system is being called upon to cope with anxieties caused by the way you have reacted to particular happenings or desires met with during your daily life. These, if easily worked upon to restore peace of mind to your general mental state, will not energise your central core stimulation centre to more than usual activity. If woken during Rapid Eye Movement sleep, you may report dreams but they are likely to be banal and forgettable. Your system is working normally to dampen down over-stimulation, encourage memory lay down, sort your memories into an easily retrievable position or relegate them to the distant past, and do all the overnight 'make and mend' that keeps you in a settled mental state by day.

Dreams caused by anxiety

However, if you have an anxiety or worry through the day that really upsets you and you have not been able to find a solution to it before bed time, then, during the make and mend time of REM sleep, the part of your brain that oversees the processes that try to make you reach peace of mind is working overtime. Bizarre dream pictures are produced that wake you and leave your waking thoughts with a powerful, tangled mass of unsorted material. Your brain, in effect, is telling you to sort out the problem during the day so that the mechanisms in your next night's REM sleep may be able to work smoothly to reach peace of mind.

Analysing your dreams

This is why you should look at your dreams, learn to analyse them and use their pictures for your own benefit. I believe dream analysis should be like keeping an eye on the daily weather forecasts. Admittedly you can't do much to change the daily weather, but forecasts show continuing patterns of cloud and fine weather sweeping across the country: in a similar way continual assessment of your dreams builds into a morning picture highlighting the previous day's problems. Regular assessment of your dreams will give you forewarning of trouble looming or reassure you that you have an unworried start to the day ahead.

You don't need to be neurotic to analyse your dreams. You don't need to go to a dream analyst if you can learn to understand what your dreams are telling you. You can do it yourself and so use your dreams in the way I believe they are meant to be used, to give you peace of mind and mental equilibrium.

If you do not take the trouble to analyse them, troublesome dreams are likely to repeat or similar dreams recur until some sort of equilibrium has been restored within your brain and your central core stimulation mechanism has regained its normal work rate.

Schizophrenia

The interesting thing about this theory is that it may also go some way to explain what happens in psychoses. If you have seen schizophrenics in an acute phase you would have been struck with how nearly they appear to be locked into a dream state. They are in a world of their own, motivated by things and people you cannot see. They speak to and about things that have no reality and, though momentarily you seem to have made contact with them, their hold on reality fades away.

This form of psychosis would be readily explained by the

theory that the brain's self-stimulation mechanism had been fixed in overdrive by some malfunctioning of the normal brain pattern of behaviour. A dream state erupts into daily life and, until it can be controlled and brought back into a normal functioning rate, sufferers are locked into a dream world from which they cannot escape and in which they may behave in a bizarre fashion.

I remember being called to a young woman who I knew as a rational, pleasant patient who had newly finished her teacher training course and had become a games mistress in a neighbourhood school. She was striding up and down her bedroom with enormous energy talking about climbing towards the magic mushrooms that she appeared to desire. Reasoning with her was hopeless. She could not sit down. She had this all-consuming need to climb towards her goal. She appeared to think she was on a hillside, searching for magic mushrooms. Her boyfriend had been half amused at first but was now as anxious as I was. I tried to break into her delusional state, telling her I wanted to take her to hospital for treatment, telling her she was not well. At times she agreed. She would say "I need help. I need help". Then she would be away again on her mountainside and unreachable by us.

She was diagnosed as having become schizophrenic. With treatment she again became the normal, pleasant person I knew. She was aware enough of having been very unhappy in her delusional state never to miss her treatment. She had no desire to relapse. Not all schizophrenics are so aware. They resent life-long treatment and often relapse because they renege on their medication. Perhaps the delusional state is not always unattractive. It is certainly difficult for their nearest and dearest and may be dangerous for them as well.

Schizophrenia usually begins in adolescence or early adult life. I saw some recent research that suggested that, at this time of turbulent hormonal change, the brain, which previously had been thought to be fully formed, appears to form new neural linkages in certain parts of the cortex and this area remains present during adolescence and then regresses thereafter. It is possible to suppose that, in some people, linkages facilitating over-activity of neuronal structures cause over-stimulation that leads to schizophrenic type psychoses.

Depression

Researchers will continue to investigate these new findings, as well as the chemical changes within the normal and abnormal brain. No one is fully aware of what happens within a brain suffering from mental disease. But theories such as the one about core self-stimulation allow you to understand what might be happening. It is the more likely because depressed patients' dreams are very different from those of non-depressed people. One could suggest that, in the depressed mind, the central system is understimulated. This is supported by the observation that depressed people have few dreams and those they report are dull and banal. Their sleep pattern is seriously disturbed by early morning wakening and an inability to get back to sleep in the later hours of the night. Using this theory you would say that they have no need of REM sleep because there is no brain self-stimulation to elicit it.

The theory is supported by the finding that a significant number of depressed people are benefited by being denied sleep, especially REM sleep, their depression often clearing quickly. This does not work for all those diagnosed as having depression, so perhaps the condition has multiple precipitating factors. In those who do benefit from it, it appears that stopping up the outflow of core self-stimulation into poor quality dreams dams up the central well in some way and allows it to function at a more normal level by day, as shown by the lifting of the depressive symptoms. Allowing unmonitored sleep may then cause a relapse. Many anti-depressive medications prevent REM sleep and some part of their beneficial action may be explained in this way.

Dreams as mental healing

There are chemical interactions and causes for brain neurones to behave in normal and abnormal ways that, when fully understood, will allow scientists to know exactly how your brain works. They are well advanced along the road already, but this psychological explanation can help you to understand what is going on in your brain. At worst, it is again the correlation of physical symptoms with theoretical ideas and perhaps closer to reality than Freud managed. There is as yet no universal theory of dream origin. Some psychologists even believe that dreams are there to make you forget problems or to prevent fantasy entering your waking life. I believe that all these theorists are working towards the same truth, that dreams are part of your brain's way of helping you to reach peace of mind.

Buddhist dream interpretation

All religions seek beneficial peace of mind under different guises. Buddhists consider dreaming a sixth sense which can be encouraged and purified by tantric exercises. Many Buddhist monks experience signs and omens of great significance through dreams.

Tibetans divide dreams into three 'Watches of the Night'. In the first Watch are those dreams occurring early in the night. These are said to be under the Karmic influence or are from the consequences of your own life. These early night dreams equate well with sleep onset dreams where your own thoughts are responsible for your entry into the dream.

In the second Watch of the Night, they say, come dreams from the influence of spirits. In the West, these dreams would include night terrors and sleepwalking, both of which could well appear as possession by an outside spirit.

In the third Watch are prophetic dreams. This has to be REM dreaming. You may not believe they are prophetic utterances from outside sources but if analysed correctly these dreams do tell you what you want to do, what you perhaps ought to do and what your feelings are about any current situation.

The Tibetans have never had a period when dreaming was against their religious tenets. They are therefore much further advanced in Dream Theory and much more able to accept the use of dreams to help with their daily life problems.

Modern approaches to dreams

Christianity has come out of the dark ages where dreams were proscribed by the priesthood and those who looked to them as useful guides to current thoughts were severely dealt with. Modern civilisation has a long way to go to catch up with the observations of people who have used dream work for hundreds of years and passed down their findings. Modern civilisation, however, has scientific expertise and the financial backing to catch up with dream research.

All countries and religions are progressing in their thinking towards the notion that, asleep or awake, you are open to the workings of your mind to your benefit or to higher endeavour. Learning to find out what your dreams mean is merely a step towards knowing yourself better and so allowing yourself to do your best. Pushing your physical self to be a great athlete, scientist or artist, or just to make the best of yourself, widens your mind; knowing yourself really well allows you to consolidate such achievements. Understanding your dreams and acting on that understanding can bring you peace of mind more readily than if you ignore them.

5

HOW TO DEAL WITH NIGHTMARES

Nightmares are one of the nastiest things to cope with during sleep, and the best known.

My own nightmare

I had not had one in years until I was asked to write this book and agreed a completion date. By day I ran around like a headless chicken wondering how I was going to complete it in time and by night I began to have anxiety dreams.

However, my continuing daytime commitments to looking after my grandchildren, finishing other articles and managing a music agency so filled the day that I was unable to settle down to reading or planning for this book. I knew I was heading for trouble and it came. On the third night of anxiety dreaming, instead of waking fully after having had a terrible dream of a high official of some kind who told me I would have to resit all my medical examinations the next day, despite my rational pleading that I needed to revise, look at text books and smarten up my knowledge, I half woke, sweating, and had enough waking time to remember saying to myself, "Oh no, here it comes", when I was gripped by sleep again and found myself walking along a hospital corridor.

Modern hospitals are all high tech, with windowed passages and pleasant decoration. Where I trained was an old Victorian hospital whose wards were light and busy if crowded, but whose internal corridors, high oblong boxes with curtained ward doors, were lit at night by forty watt bulbs that left a shadowy effect. In my dream it was darker even than that. The greenish paint on the walls did not help. It was not a corridor I knew, but it was familiar. There were doors off it, presumably into wards, but I felt hesitant to take them. I did not know what was on the other side of the doors and they had no numbers or nameplates. They were not for me. As I went on, the corridor narrowed and became less high. I could suddenly sense something very frightening behind me. I started to hurry but I found I could not. I was walking in treacle. Nothing would move though I struggled to run. The weight on my chest became huge, pressing me down, and the something behind me was very very close.

As I was making a superhuman effort to move I woke with a jerk, panting and shaking, and still afraid. My heart was beating fifteen to the dozen. After doing one of my immediate first aid manoeuvres to alleviate the nightmare, I let myself wake fully, back into my own world. Looking at the time, I found that, though it was early, I could get up without too much comment. I did so. I wasn't going to risk another nightmare. I went straight to my books on sleep and dreaming and started to read. I was not going to allow the next night to produce a nightmare if I could help it.

That experience is very typical and shows many of the features that precipitate, occur during, and can prevent nightmares. I believe a nightmare is the final and strongest message your brain can send you to say that you need to clean up your mental act by day. You are being told unequivocally that you have some monumental hang-up due to anxiety, resentment, or guilt that you are not dealing with and need to.

The universality of nightmares

The interesting thing about nightmares is that they are so universal, so similar and have been so well documented since dreams were first talked about and that is at least three thousand years.

Everyone knows the horror of having a nightmare. It is the dream that turns into a terrifying experience with monsters, dreadful people or just a menacing presence that is never seen, creeping up upon you as you try to get away.

Being unable to run

Whereas in dreams you can move freely, in nightmares you often cannot. You try to run but your legs won't move or move so slowly and with so much effort that you can scarcely cover ground. As you already know, messages to your brain in REM sleep are attenuated and changed, but I believe that this feeling of being unable to move comes from the flaccid paralysis that your limbs are affected with in REM sleep. They could not move if they wanted to. This message is getting through to your higher centres and is being interpreted this way in your dream. Your terror mounts. You feel an enormous pressure on your chest and you can hardly breathe though you are gasping for air. Like the feeling of limb paralysis, I believe this feeling of suffocation comes from messages to your brain telling you that the ancillary muscles of breathing, between your ribs and in your shoulder girdle, are immobile in REM sleep, just as your limbs are.

Usually just as you are about to be engulfed by whatever is after you, you wake, sometimes with a wild movement or a scream as your voice and limbs become unlocked with wakening.

The difference between nightmares and night terrors

Nightmares, as I explained on page 37, are not night terrors. Night terrors arise in the deeper stages of non-REM sleep, usually earlier in the night. Nightmares occur in REM sleep, usually towards the end of the night and they are slow to build and terrifying for the dreamer who is well aware of his experience when he wakes.

Nightmares are not forgettable. They stay with you and, if recurrent, make you unhappy about going to sleep. They may be so frightening and threatening that they overwhelm your mind by day, blotting out the anxiety or guilt that caused them in the first place with a growing apprehension as the day draws in that you will have to face another night with its attendant horror.

The meaning of the word 'nightmare'

The second half of the word 'nightmare' has nothing to do with horses. It comes from the Old English word 'Mara', a monster from Hell who, in mediaeval times, was thought to range round the country by night and, where possible, enter your bedroom while you slept, leaping upon your unresisting form and pressing on your chest to suffocate and attack you or, if you were a woman, rape you. If you woke, 'Mara' was scared off. Our ancestors, who believed this story, woke feeling that they had had a narrow escape. That feeling of relief at being still alive after a nightmare still affects you to this day though without needing to believe in spectres.

A visitation by "the night hag" or "a riding of the witch" were phrases people of that time used to describe a nightmare. The French word for it is "cauchemar", the "fiend who tramples".

With the ever present fear of being thought to be associating with hell-spawned beings and the threat of suffering the cleansing fire that the clergy and judiciary of the Middle Ages thought an appropriate deterrent, the common or garden man or woman did not talk about their nightmares. It was never wise to let Mother Church know that you had any communication with witches, however inadvertent or unwelcome. If you were thought to be a medium that allowed the wickedness of hell fire through into your community, you had to go. All Mother Church's punishments tended to stress you to destruction. The theories of the time held that, if you were burned or drowned and really were a witch, you were purged. If you were not, you were better off in heaven anyway and your unmerited punishment had merely got you there faster.

People put up with bad dreams, especially nightmares. They kept the horror to themselves and therefore little work was done to alleviate them until after Freud and his fellow psychoanalysts brought dreaming back into the symptomatology of medicine and therefore made nightmares an acceptable thing to complain about to your doctor.

Dealing with your nightmares

There is no reason to continue to keep your nightmares to yourself, to fear each night in case one visits you. It is not necessary to put up with nightmares. A nightmare, as I said earlier, is the final stage in continuing dreams, usually of anxiety and fear, but also of guilt and possibly anger and resentment. Most people can remember dreams of anxiety in the nights before a nightmare and can pinpoint that anxiety which they have not managed to alleviate through the day.

Pinpointing the cause of your anxiety

The nightmare, when it comes, does not usually highlight that anxiety or guilt as the preceding dreams do. It is a strong statement that something must be done by day to get rid of anxiety and it usually uses fears and memories from childhood to illustrate its message.

Your dream picture of where you are is not real. To take the nightmare I described as illustration, I was not in a hospital. However I have walked long darkened corridors like the ones in my nightmare when I was an intern, to use the

American phraseology, and though I cannot remember ever having felt alarmed in them, that setting is one that recurs in my nightmares. It almost certainly comes out of childhood memories of fear in darkened passages.

Recognising signs in nightmares

I was brought up in Sri Lanka and the bungalow I lived in had cement verandas all round it. They were unlit except for the light shining from inside through rooms' windows, and as we made our own electricity this was dim enough even inside the bungalow. The night is very dark around an isolated house on a rubber plantation and the trees and night sounds press in. As a small child maybe they frightened me. I cannot recall it, but when I think about the hospital corridor I am reminded of the bungalow floors, so similar to the walls and floors of the corridor. I have always felt nervous about going into strange environments. It doesn't stop me doing it. I often even enjoy the excitement, but I do remember feeling continually lost when I first went to school and just following the crowd more in hope than expectation that it was right.

My best friend once said, "The only reason you ended up in the first set for everything was that you followed me around and the mistress just thought it was too much effort to get you to the right class." She may have been right. It never fussed me. It is the way I am. But my brain knows what frightens me and when it needs to tell me that I am so far from peace of mind that only a nightmare will do to get me moving it usually produces a feeling of being pursued by an unpersonified fearfulness in a half lit, narrow area of some kind. It is not that I am claustrophobic in any recognisable way: these feelings are under control. In nightmares, they escape to make a significant point. Now that I know what to do about them, the nightmare is even more effective in getting me to rectify the situation.

Affirmative action
In the first instance, as soon as I woke I retreated into relaxation and the retrieval of some fragments of sleep and summoned up the picture of the long corridor, the shadowy threatening doorways and the feeling of pursuit. I then took myself through the nearest door and peopled the room with doctors from my student year, all working at their various tasks. I joined them and felt safe. When I left the room it was with a friend and the corridor had become bright, the threat gone, and it was daytime, time to wake fully. This was not what is called ''lucid dreaming'', which is described on page 36. This was daydreaming in a sleep stage more akin to that reached in Transcendental Meditation or early sleep onset, probably between sleep Stage 1 and 2. It is, however, a very effective way to turn off serial nightmares, or at least mitigate the remaining horror, especially for children.

Fighting back
Another way to alleviate nightmares is to use the same technique of remaining asleep but attack your aggressor and vanquish it. Give yourself a weapon or a shield or a flame-thrower and blast whatever is creeping up on you. Children sometimes find this technique attractive.

Children's nightmares
Children do seem to have nightmares, especially when faced with a serious anxiety. We adults expect our young to take new situations in their stride. But a new school, going camping with a school group or on a project with other children they are not comfortable with, and of course the continuing hurdle of examinations that perhaps they feel less than prepared for, are all stressful occasions which may provoke anxiety and, thereafter, nightmares. Home situations where there is bereavement or the instability and noisy recriminations of a marital break-up are even more severe stressors. Children are so powerless.

They must feel frightened many times.

If the stress is transitory, the nightmares will stop after the stress is gone. In fact, if the child does well in the test he feared or enjoyed the camp he was apprehensive of, he will be more confident when facing a new challenge. If the experience was horrendous, it leaves a pathway for more rapid recurrences of the same sort of horrors if stress returns.

The impact of TV violence

These days, with television characters, both real and cartoon, locked in mortal conflict with every kind of monster, there is no shortage of dream content for a child's nightmare. They need not just fear advancing darkness closing in on them. These days, children's nightmares are full of blood pouring all over themselves, weapons of destruction and some very fancy monsters. Commonly a cartoon seen the evening before is involved.

Bullying

One six-year-old child I know told me that he had had a bad dream. His brother was trying to tear his eyes out, he said, and then the fire brigade van came but it went back and forward, back and forward and side to side until it squashed him flat as he ran about trying to escape from it. He was suffering bullying from his younger brother who was rightly shown in his nightmare in an aggressive role. As for the fire engine, the day before the dream the fire department had visited the school and his class had been very close to their big red crane van.

It was clearly time to bring the bullying into the open and get his parents to discuss it with both children and put a stop to it. I told him that if he was pursued by anything big in his dreams ever again he was to pretend he had a magic skateboard that would whisk him home, even through the air if necessary.

Teaching children to fight back

Children are mostly very ready to daydream a huge sword into their hands to behead a monster, or imagine a magic carpet at their feet to soar out of reach. They will draw their monsters and cut them out and play with them till they become familiar and non-frightening denizens of the night. In fact, they are just turning their nightmare figures into cartoon characters like the ones they may see on any television programme. They learn how to deal with them. For a child, familiarity breeds, if not contempt, contentment.

One seven year old I know had nightmares about skeletons chasing him in the dark. The only significant thing that I knew had recently happened in the family was that his younger brother had been diagnosed as having a bone disease and had had to have an operation. The older boy had gone with his mother and brother to hospital and had been present when the doctor had shown his mother the X-rays. The little chap hadn't liked them. He was, however, perfectly happy to consider digging a ditch behind him as the skeletons came at him and he told me he felt much better when they all fell into his ditch and could not get out. That nightmare did not return. Of course, his mother and I took the opportunity of going over the whole story of his brother's problem with him, explaining that the doctors had made his brother better with the operation and that it was very bad luck that it had happened to his brother but was something that would not affect him.

Childhood anxieties

Children's nightmares have a very blurred border with bad anxiety dreams. They do not have classical adult nightmares. Rather, they find themselves in dreadful situations whose material comes from something that they have seen or something that they have experienced in the previous twenty-four hours.

One young child told me about a dream where he had just come off a plane and was sitting in his school's basketball court with all of his luggage. Someone came and took some of it away and he went after them to get it back but all the time worried about what was happening to the luggage he had had to leave when he gave chase. He had just been on a plane journey and his anxieties were showing. He told me that all his dreams came from things he had done or seen the previous day. I believe this is normal for most people but especially for children, so it becomes very important what your children see on television before they go to bed. Horror films will beget horror dreams. If your children want to see a really scary movie don't let it be last thing at night.

More ways of dealing with nightmares

Another immediate technique to mitigate nightmares is just to lie quiet and allow the dark destroyer to catch up with you and overtake you, envelope you and then drain away like a miasma. It will not do this in the nightmare, but only if you let it in the daydream afterwards, and you may then lie there and say to yourself, "See, it didn't really hurt, did it? I am still here". Some people facing the nightmare that follows diagnosis of a serious illness, and with a need to achieve resignation and acceptance, prefer to use this last method. It is not everybody's preference as it seems to allow the nightmare to win. However, it does allow the brain to switch off the nightmare scenario for long enough to reach some sort of peace of mind.

Whichever method you use depends on your own mental makc up and psychological preference. The usual one is the first one I described and that is the one I always use. It alleviates the horror.

Dealing with anxieties

The second stage of treating a nightmare is to find the anxiety and deal with it. The nightmare itself does not always give clues as to what the precipitating problem is. It merely gives you a really frightening time and allows you to wake upset and remember the fear so that you will be motivated to do something about it: punishment by your brain, if you like, for not having cleared the causative problem earlier.

If you look again at the dreams I was having before the nightmare their message was perfectly clear. I wish all dreams carried such a simple message. I even verbalised the problem to my examining agent. ''I need time to work and prepare for my examination,'' I complained in the dream. ''How can you expect me to do well if I don't get a chance to revise?'' I felt a sense of unfairness in his insisting that I must sit the exam without the preparation I desired, as well as a sense of being unprepared; this despite the fact that the deadline had been my initiative, not my publisher's. It interested me that my brain seemed to carry a monitoring duty that checked my waking brain's decisions and was able to warn against them if it thought they had been unrealistic.

This sort of overview is, I believe, part of the conscience mechanism that we build through childhood to oversee our behaviour. We may override it by day and do things that we know are not right and we are not comfortable with but ignore our better feelings. By night these feelings are not under our control and our offence is brought to mind in dreams.

I allayed mine by hard work and making a start on the book so that my anxiety dreams stopped and, thank goodness, the nightmares with them.

Post Traumatic Stress Disorder

A particular form of nightmare is found with Post Traumatic Stress Disorder, where someone has seen or been part of something so terrible, so frightening and so abnormal, that they have been overwhelmed by the experience. An example is being the only survivor in a car crash, being a rape victim or witnessing a murder. Soldiers in action see and participate in horrors that remain with them. Every war has thrown up men who could not forget the dreadfulness. In the First World War doctors called it 'shell shock'. In the Second World War it was 'battle fatigue'. Post Traumatic Stress describes the condition better. The sufferer has flashbacks of the incident or incidents which can occur at any time, but often at night when he has nightmares that are severe and recurring and may make the sufferer unwilling to attempt sleep. This further exacerbates the condition.

Behind the condition is often an answering childhood fear that is exacerbated by the episode. There is also a hefty dollop of guilt and anxiety. The anxiety is understandable, but the guilt less so. It is often totally irrational. A rape victim will feel that she could have done more to prevent the attack, perhaps even fear, in retrospect, that she initiated the response. The same happens with a car crash. The survivor, instead of feeling lucky to be alive, feels that in some way he is at fault because he is the survivor. In war, this irrational guilt is even more marked. "Why did I live through it when my friends died beside me?"

In a smaller way, some heart bypass or transplant patients are unable to assimilate their good fortune. Patients have said to me, "I was really dead for quite a while. I can't accept that I am alive again."

Eliminating guilt

It is essential in all these cases to eliminate these irrational feelings of guilt and anxiety attached to the episode before trying to disperse the nightmare. They may not all be completely irrational. Perhaps a car crash survivor had some unease about himself as a driver. Was he tired? Had he drunk any alcohol in the previous few hours that could have affected him? Was his eyesight as good as when he was younger? Could he have noticed that child running off the pavement earlier?

It is so easy to blame yourself after an event, even if no one else is doing so. It takes specialist therapy in many cases to make you comfortable with yourself after a traumatic episode, and it is worth seeking it early so that healing is not delayed. Thereafter, the nightmares may cease of their own accord or you can take medication for a short time that suppresses REM sleep and so leaves you confident of relaxed, dream-free sleep. If nightmares recur, you may attempt the short-term treatments of nightmare that I have outlined in this chapter and, in the longer term, look for some hidden anxiety, which may or may not be related to the event that precipitated the Post Traumatic Stress Disorder. There is little point trying to cure the nightmares first. It seldom works.

Generally, it is thought that those who suffer PTSD have in their past a fear that is mirrored by the feelings of the traumatic event. Perhaps, in childhood, the sufferer of a car crash has hated speed and used to feel ''Stop! Stop! I can't stand this''. The crash itself, if speeding was to blame, brings out all that well hidden and forgotten fear and begets the guilt that says, ''You should have insisted on going slower. Then everyone would be alive.'' This despite the fact that he probably did ask for a slower speed and was ignored. Guilt is irrational and damaging. It needs to be assuaged by full exposure and you yourself pardoning yourself because you see clearly that you could have done no more than you did in that circumstance.

Enjoying a nightmare

Some people like to live dangerously and enjoy their nightmares, even make them work for them. Artists and poets and authors have been known to welcome them to provide inspiration. Not for them are the techniques to turn off the experience. Some of the more alarming works of art I have seen might well have had their origin in a nightmare.

Predispositions towards nightmares

If nightmares are a recurring lifelong experience for you, and you have grown used to them, you are likely to have an open trusting nature and a creative artistic mind. Literature suggests that you are the sort of person who is more gullible and likely to be taken advantage of, as well as being more sensitive to life's stresses and therefore more readily upset by reverses of any kind. It is not that you are more phobic, or fearful or hostile. It is more that you are thin skinned. Rigid, solid obsessional characters are not usually so affected by nightmares. Their way is clear to them and other people's feelings are not so important to them. They are more self-absorbed.

If nightmares have been your constant companion, consider a long look at yourself. Do you need a course in self-assertion? Do you need to strengthen your own sense of self? Should you encourage your ability in an artistic field and, in that way, give yourself the self-confidence and knowledge that sets you free from vulnerability? Above all, look at your nightmares in depth and try to remember if they are highlighting any childhood episode of vulnerability or fear. So often some episode in childhood can be remembered and from an adult perspective may be both understood and dispersed.

A female friend who suffered nightmares remembered being five years old and standing with her mother at a railway station, waiting for the train that was bringing her father home after an absence of a year. Her mother was clearly over the moon with excitement but she, who wanted to be as happy, was terrified that she would not recognise him and he would be disappointed.

In the event it did not matter as his identity was made plain by her mother leaping into this big male's arms, and then she was hugged in her turn and was happy to be loved. But that feeling of anxiety coloured much of her childhood, she told me. She always felt vulnerable before new jobs, parties with new people, new places to go to and often had nightmares before these things, although afterwards it all worked out and the nightmares did not recur. Strengthening her self confidence and allowing her to understand her anxieties about how she would manage in unfamiliar situations, and finding techniques for her to use so that the old memories of insecurity could be forgotten, produced fewer nightmares, as well as increasing her day time enjoyment of new challenges.

Living with nightmares

Nightmares are classified as sleep disorders, unlike anxiety dreams which are not. They tend to decrease in intensity and frequency with age, although women continue to report them into a later age than men. Perhaps men become more self confident with age? Male and female children report nightmares with the same frequency.

Medication

Nightmares may be caused by medication, especially the levodopa derivatives that are given to allay the tremor of Parkinsonism. Some beta-blockers, usually given for high blood pressure and angina, may also on occasion precipitate nightmares. These are especially significant because they have anxiolytic properties and may be prescribed to allay anxiety. If you suddenly start having nightmares after starting a new medicine you should enquire from your doctor if it could be the cause.

Psychosis

Vivid, frightening, escalating dreaming may precede a psychotic episode, especially if associated with increasing insomnia. If you are in contact with a person who has had either schizophrenia or manic depression, and is in remission or is well controlled, a change for the worse in their sleep pattern, accompanied by nightmares, should sound a warning bell and suggest that a visit to the doctor is advisable to recheck their treatment efficacy.

6

DREAMS OF FEELINGS AND EMOTIONS

My dream

Just before I woke I saw a single dark swallow high in the air, outlined against a pale sky, and I woke to the thought, "Oh, good. It is going to be a fine day." The rest of the dream was lost. The very act of concentration on that one part of it allowed the rest to slide out of my memory, though I tried to go after it like a man trying to lift a fish from a stream with his hand. It was an instance of what Freud called 'extrinsic stimulation' causing dream pictures, with the effect of light on my retina telling my brain something. It was certainly not a memory of the previous night's weather forecast, which was for showers and blustery winds. It was not even very important to me, which perhaps was why the rest of the dream was lost. It was just another day and fine weather might mean a comfortable round of golf but also watering the garden, while wet weather would let me off the latter but probably offer something other than an outdoor sport.

For me, swallows flying high betoken good weather in the offing. Something in the quality of light coming through my bedroom blind and closed eyelids must have triggered my retina and, through it, my brain to recognise a sunny day in the making. The tail end of my dream picked up the stimulation, offering me a picture I would understand.

To many people, swallows could mean something quite different. Dream books suggest that birds mean you will go on a long journey. Psychoanalysts might suggest that they meant my desire to escape from my current lifestyle, or get away from my parents or family. They might want to dig deeply into my relationships with my nearest and dearest.

Analysing your own dreams

This is why you should learn to analyse your own dreams. You really are the only person who can accurately assess and interpret them. You know where to start and when to stop. For me, this was a simple picture of recognising a good day in the offing with a feeling of general well being, waking comfortably without pain or anxiety or desire for immediate action. I did not feel I needed to take that dream any further. I had recognised a good day in the making and my general attitude to it was welcoming.

Your experiences and memories

To start at the beginning of dream interpretation you first need to know that you only ever dream of things you have seen or experienced at some time. Some memories may be from babyhood or childhood and you may have no recollection of the exact episode or when it happened. However, people who are blind from birth do not dream in pictures. In fact, if they become blind at up to about five years old their dreams usually become attenuated on the visual front until that part of the dream almost disappears from their adult dreams. If they become blind after that age, their dreams do continue to contain visual material, occurring right on so that twenty or thirty years later they may have a dream where they can see. In the same way, those people who have been deaf from birth have silent dreams.

What goes on in dreams may well be a sorting out of

memories, a categorisation and re-siting of those memories to reflect their importance as you go through life with new experiences and cognitive effort supplanting thoughts previously important to you.

It almost appears as if memory is painted onto the surface of your brain's memory store, and so if one memory is triggered strongly enough the ones next door may also be activated. As these are stored in an order that you have no apparent waking control over, you get the bizarre coming together of various apparently unrelated pictures and adventures in your dream. There is little you can do about that and it is not significant. What is worth looking at is what your overall feeling is within and after the dream.

Repetitive dreams

A patient came to see me with a repetitive dream that was troubling her. She was a district nurse who had a little girl of about three years old. She was happily married and I had always thought of her as sensible and well adjusted.

However, she told me that she had started to dream of being in a maternity hospital awaiting a caesarean section. She explained that in her dream she was on the operating table with a green-draped screen in front of her face to prevent her seeing the surgeons at work. When the dream began she had had an epidural anaesthetic, which had completely paralysed her legs. The surgeons were about to start when she realised that, although her legs were unable to move, the anaesthetic had not completely taken hold and she could feel her abdomen. Realising that her doctors were about to make an incision she tried to stop them. No one listened. She could see the surgeons getting their scalpels ready to cut through her abdominal wall and she struggled to tell the nurse standing by her head that she was not prepared for the operation. The nurse made soothing noises and told her to relax. She said she struggled to move but could not. She called out to anyone who could hear but no one was listening. The green-gowned surgeon still approached and, as he began the operation, she woke.

I knew she was hoping to have a second child. She had had the first by caesarean section and so her dream memories were extremely accurate about the operating theatre, the screens in front of her face and the nurse beside her. As she was not a midwife she had probably never been in an obstetric operating theatre otherwise, so her dream material came from accurate observation when she had her first baby. That first birth had been no problem to her. She might not have enjoyed the process but she had experienced no pain or unease and was looking forward to having her second baby the same way.

Now she wondered if she was beginning to fear having another child. She could not think why she might have suddenly become nervous about a process that had been so pain free and simple. She explained that she did not want these dreams to pursue her for the next nine months and asked if she could have been traumatised by the event and not noticed it.

Dreams highlighting apparently unrelated anxieties

''Were you anxious in the dream?'' I asked. She thought about that and answered slowly. ''No. No. I was not nervous or anxious at all. I was annoyed with them for not listening to me and I felt completely frustrated and helpless to do anything about it. No one would listen to me, not the nurse, not anyone. I knew they were going to make a mistake and give me trouble but would they listen to me? No.''

''What is it that is frustrating you to such a degree just now?'' I asked. ''Oh . . . Is that all?'' Her face cleared and she got up to go. ''I'm so glad it was only that. I thought I was getting psychologically disturbed.''

I could not let her away without explanation and slightly shame-facedly she told me that her neighbour had died recently. The old lady had been befriended by the whole tenement in which she lived and my patient used to go to see her with her little girl and bring her food on occasion. Her death was a sadness to them all. However, the little girl's birthday was that week, the week of the funeral, and my patient had planned a party for her with some of her friends. Her neighbours, hearing her plans, were telling her that she should not hold it. It was not appropriate, they said. She had become very frustrated about this as she did not feel that her daughter would understand her reasons for cancelling her party and she would be upset and disappointed. She did not see why the little girl should be made miserable by something that had no real affect on her. She was however sensitive to her neighbours' feelings and so she found herself in a quandary and frustration was her overriding reaction.

"Take the children to the Zoo," I suggested. "That way no one needs to know that you are having a party. Take the cake to the cafeteria."

Once she realised the cause of the dream and changed her plans for her party, her frustration that her neighbours were not seeing her side of her problem disappeared. Her dream did not recur either. She rang to tell me so, as well as mentioning that the Zoo party had been a great success.

In her case, the vivid pictures her brain was producing could have betokened anxiety or even a nightmare. Only she was aware that the main feeling was frustration. It was this frustration that her dream mind was trying to tell her to sort out by day. The feeling was too strong, too overwhelming, to be relieved by the simple dreaming and storing system that goes on, I believe, every night in REM sleep in order to provide peace of mind the next day.

Finding a link in your anxieties

She might have gone further into her dream to consider whether there was an element of being afraid of another pregnancy, with its attendant caesarean delivery. It would be normal for her to have some reservations. Dreams of birth might have some relevance to a fear of death, brought to mind by the death of her neighbour. The feeling that life is passing by at a great rate occurs to everyone when death touches one of your friends. But she was not unnaturally upset by these thoughts. She could accept that these events had a part in the pictures of her dream, but they were not a key factor. As a professional nurse who had given up her job for a time to bring up her young daughter, she might have wondered if she was frustrated by no longer being a person of importance in her own right. All these feelings may have had some part of her dream picture, but they were not significant and she was aware of this. She knew at once what her main overwhelming frustration was at that time. That she was correct in her interpretation was proved when the dream did not return after she changed her plans for her little girl's party. There seemed no need to delve further in to her thought processes, to stir up material that had been suppressed or sublimated to allow her peace of mind for her daily life. She did not want to either, hence her relief when curing her frustration stopped the dreaming.

Exploring your own dreams

You can fish as far as you like within your dreams, finding material and thoughts that you can mull over and sort out to your satisfaction. You will find feelings from long ago that you are now able to accept or understand from the perspective of perhaps several years of maturation. You can take the simple obvious message and deal with it to achieve peace of mind and allow your REM sleep to continue its routine chores without overload.

Signals to your true feelings

Another thing your dreams do is to tell you your true feelings. You may have rationalised them away into some sensible attitude and decided that some wish that you had was irrational or unnecessary, but if it was a strong desire it will resurface at dream time.

I can remember seeing a Bokhara rug in a carpet shop. I thought it beautiful. I wanted it. I even went in and asked the price. I couldn't readily afford it. It wouldn't have been a disaster if I had bought it, but it wasn't a necessity either. No one else in the family felt much about it either way so it did seem fairly silly to insist on buying it. I don't carry long term desires once I have decided not to indulge them and I just forgot the whole thing in the hurly burly of everyday family life. That sort of thought just disappears amid the more urgent ones of what to buy for the next meal and whether the washing needs ironing. A week later I dreamed I saw that carpet in its window and I could feel it in my hands and adore its every pattern and change of colour and I woke lusting after it in a way I had not realised I felt even at the time.

Somewhere deep in my mind I had wanted that carpet more than I had realised and having dreamed it I recognised the deep desire. Luckily a birthday was looming and I knew what I wanted to ask for and that carpet has given me nothing but joy ever since. But for that dream, I would never have possessed it.

''What superficial dreams you have,'' say my friends. That may be so. I believe most people have uncomplicated dreams that are very easily interpreted by themselves. The pictures may be convoluted and complex but the theme should be clear to you.

'Chasing' dreams

A television producer on the up and up in the media world once told me that he had repeated dreams of chasing things.

On one night he was pursuing tigers through snow-clad hills, another he was chasing a train that was just leaving the station.

My question, "What do you feel in your dreams?" was answered by, "I am just desperate to get whatever it is that I am chasing."

"Is there a special job coming up?" Of course there was. The director of his film unit was moving on and he badly wanted the post. "Do your best to make yourself the best person for the job," I advised. "Then you won't be so anxious and absorbed with longing for it."

He may have followed my advice, but his dreams persisted on and off until he got the job. They did not recur afterwards.

Freud suggested that dreams of trying to catch trains or sit exams stem from your fear of death. When you miss them or arrive too late for the exam you heave a sigh of relief and say to yourself, "Death missed me that time. I am so happy that I have not been carried off or made to face a severe trial."

This is producing a universal diagnosis for an occurrence that has to be different for each person. I cannot agree with this sort of rationalisation. It is too close to 'subject diagnosis' of dreams. I believe that most people running for a train in their dreams are experiencing just the sort of despairing pursuit that they would in their daytime life. That is the feeling the dream is trying to put across. There may also be hints in the dream as to what the dreamer really wants, if the dreamer is not already well aware of his or her current desire. My friend was, but the scenes of chasing tigers in the snow were so pictorial that they had to come from his working life where he made pictures for his television company, and pursuing the train to work also obviously stemmed from his occupational activity rather than the home.

We all occasionally fear death in the watches of the night and have worked out mechanisms for overcoming this very normal apprehension. I do not think that this anxiety is only ever associated with dreams of trains and examinations which are much more likely to be anxiety related, not necessarily to do with death.

Examination dreams

When I first started work on this book, years ago, I dreamed that I was entering my final medical examination with all my friends. They all seemed perfectly content, but I complained to them all that we had sat it years ago and, to do it justice, I needed to read more about it because I had forgotten all the rarer conditions that I might need to discuss in my paper. This was a dream of similar circumstances to the one I had when contemplating my deadline, but predated it by at least five years. It would have been easy for someone who did not know me to think it meant the same. It did not. It was different in that, in the first dream, I knew I needed to do more reading to sit the exam, and when I woke I put the writing of my book aside until I had done a great deal more research. It was a dream that showed me the gaps in my knowledge. The later dream was one of frustration that I had too many other commitments in my life, and anxiety that I had set myself too tight a deadline. However, once I started revising and writing after the second dream, my mind was more peaceful and similarly I had no problems with the first short draft once my brain accepted I had done enough research.

Using the messages in these dreams

Dreams can help you choose. Your waking mind may rationalise and dissect pros and cons but in REM sleep you get a clear picture of what your preferences are that stays with you into your wakening and should be looked at seriously. It is not to say that your rational waking mind should not make the decision. You just need to be aware that in dreams what your heart wants or fears is shown.

These fears may come from memories very far back in your childhood and be children's fears that need to be looked at, understood, but not necessarily given in to in your decision-making for your adult life.

Stress

Dreams of fear and being pursued are anxiety dreams. They do not have to be as acute as nightmares, which are the classic response to acute or great anxiety. Many people are just chronically overstressed and a little anxious, always running all day to keep up, a little late for everything but keeping it going. You are likely to dream that you can never get to something that is always a little ahead. If you have a fear of being found wanting and being caught out as unable to complete your day's work, you will dream of being hunted by something or someone. It might be a car or a lion or a dog, but it is always about to catch up with you and you are ducking and weaving to stay ahead. This is not the crushing fear of the nightmare, just a continuing need to stay ahead of the posse.

Mothers who are running a household and family and trying to hold down a job are a classic example of this, and may well have these kinds of dreams, as may workers who are being forced to do more than they can complete in a day. The cure is to sit down and restructure or renegotiate the amount of work you have to do so that you do not finish the day feeling hunted or pursued.

Bereavement

In bereavement as well as anxiety dreams you may waken with a great feeling of loss and sorrow. This is a natural part of adjusting to your unhappy situation. Let the loss pour over you and accept it at the time of waking, but, as you lie there, gradually turn your mind to something that you can do that day that will bring you pleasure. Find something attractive to do or someone pleasant that you like to talk to. Allow the sorrow and accept it as part of you, but let your mind have something to look forward to.

Anger

Anger is another emotion that your dreams may pinpoint. If you have allowed a deep anger or resentment about something or someone to develop, you are likely to dream of fights where you lash out or shout your fury aloud. All these negative emotions stand between you and peace of mind, and your dreams, in their work to store and cool daytime emotional volcanoes, will show you where the trouble lies.

Happiness

You can also have great feelings of happiness in dreams. These positive dreams are less common than those with negative feelings. This is natural because anxiety, anger and frustration are strong negative emotions that overwhelm your waking mind and seriously disturb your dreaming brain in its work to achieve peace of mind for you by morning. If it cannot complete the job of mitigating these feelings by wake-up time, you are handed them as a dream you remember. Even then, there is often some softening of the acute feelings you had the previous day.

Meeting old friends

Waking after a dream where you have met old friends and relations, some long dead perhaps, and talked with them and discussed old and happy times is a relaxation and a pleasure. You often manage to say to them the things you were unable to say in life about how fond you were of them. You wake with a sense of relief and satisfaction at having told them your thoughts.

Behind these dreams must be a wish that you had

explained your feelings to them when they were still with you. There must be a frustration that you have bottled up your affection and not shown it to them, a fear that they never knew how much you appreciated them. This way of resolving the situation gives you a sense of joy to wake to and you should accept it fully. If you can still let your feelings be known it might be wise to do so; if not, you should treat the experience as a catharsis, accepting that you would have liked to have made sure that your love was known and appreciated but also that they probably knew about it anyway.

Sometimes in these dreams you get advice, the sort of advice you know your loved ones would give. You wake, thinking, ''That's sound advice.'' It is worth looking at these thoughts. They do not come from someone else. The thoughts are your own and may be what you secretly want. Accept that dreams offer simplistic messages. They do not all have to be shredded to get their meaning.

Misplaced worries

Recently, I was regretting having accepted an invitation to a daylong meeting with people I did not know very well. I was interested in the subject they were discussing and I wanted to hear the lecturer but, after having accepted, I began to realise I would probably spend a whole day with strangers, with nothing to talk to them about, all for an hour of lecture that I did want to hear. It meant taking a day off work too and, as a busy General Practitioner, that was also a nuisance with clinics to make up the day after and the guilt of having to leave my partners to fill in for me. As the day approached I began to wish I had never accepted. The night before, my doubts surfaced. I dreamed I was being imprisoned with a group of people I did not know for a fault I had not any knowledge of. I was unable to escape. I had to do what I was told. That dream pinpointed my feelings absolutely. In fact, it was completely wrong. When I got to the meeting, with my dream thoughts still strong in my mind, I was surprised and delighted to meet several people I did know. The lecture was as interesting as I had hoped it would be and the day was a great pleasure and an unaccustomed relaxation in a busy life. The dream did not return and I felt a fool at having stirred it up and given myself a bad night.

Dealing with anxieties by day

I believe your waking feelings are the most important stimuli for your dreams. They become the bits thrown up by your dreaming brain in picture form as things you should be looking at with your day time mind because the thoughts or emotions are too strong to be filed away in the 'forget it' zone of your memory bank. These strong feelings need processing, ameliorating and sorting, just as a bulging file in an office needs tidying before it is put away.

Once these troubling thoughts cease to bother your brain by day, or are sufficiently acceptable to file and forget, the dreaming brain will deal with them. Until then, it is, "Take a memo, Miss Smith," and a dream that you remember, highlighting the problem, is offered to you. If you like, you get the 'punch line' of an unsortable memory as you wake from the dream that has tried to file it away.

I remember struggling through a dream of frustration, trying to circumnavigate a wallow of elephants thrashing about in a river. This is not as bizarre as it sounds. Elephants wallowing around in a river were not an uncommon sight in my childhood in Sri Lanka and, though I had never tried to push through a group of these huge unwieldy pachyderms, it did give me a clear picture of the danger and anxiety I felt as they got in my way. My husband was with me, trying to show me the way, a way I did not want to take but he kept pushing me in that direction and as we stood together I put my head on his shoulder and said, "I don't know what I would do without you,'' and woke.

I do not recall what particular frustration I was facing, but I came from that dream with a clear reinforcement of what my true feelings were for my companion through life. When I thought about it in the morning I could only be grateful to my dreaming brain for reminding me of his unfailing support and showing me someone to turn to for help in my predicament. It might even have been a reminder to my waking brain to mention occasionally to him that I loved him and relied on him. These simple courtesies get forgotten in the hurly-burly of family and working life and yet they are very much a part of maintaining a good relationship.

7

DREAMS FROM INTRINSIC AND EXTRINSIC STIMULI

A typical extrinsically-stimulated dream

A patient reported dreaming that he was driving a sports car down a deep lane with bushes on either side, like those sunken lanes you find in Scotland and Cornwall, where the brambles and wild flowers are pushed up, supported by hedges of hawthorn or deciduous saplings. It was summer, he thought, because the air was warm as it rushed by his open topped car and the hedges were green with leaves. He sat at ease at the wheel with his elbow on the top of the door, sticking out the side of the car. Suddenly, as he raced along, his arm became entangled in the bushes alongside and was drawn up above his head and torn off at the shoulder.

At this point he woke, breathless and alarmed, to find he had moved his right arm up to lie curled above his head and his newly acquired kitten, seeking comfort and warmth, had crept into his bed and was licking his armpit with its rough little tongue. The strong purr of the tiny animal had furnished the car noise of his dream; the feeling of its rasping tongue the avulsion, and the position of his arm in bed was also reproduced in his dream material.

This scenario is typical of those dreams that are caused by external stimuli. They last as long as the stimulation and they usually end in waking, caused by the stimulation, so they are remembered.

Heightened sensory awareness during sleep

When you go to sleep you are very undefended, and in REM sleep, where most of your muscles lie paralysed, you are particularly vulnerable. As if to make up for this, any unexpected sensation you feel at this time is translated into greatly magnified scenarios in your dreaming brain, which puts you into a state of emergency from which you wake.

The above dream exemplifies your ability to make mountains out of molehills in your dreaming brain. The sensations were hugely exaggerated and yet faithfully reproduced. They provided a warning to the helpless dreaming body and woke it up.

Scientists in sleep laboratories have presented all sorts of stimuli to sleeping volunteers in REM sleep and then woken them up to get their dream story. A favourite stimulus is to drip water on the volunteer's back. Some dreamers report that they have been caught in a thunderstorm, some that the roof was leaking, and some that they have fallen in the sea.

Other experimenters have allowed a dreamer's arm to lie cold outside the bedclothes. This led the volunteer to report dreams of having caught his arm in a freezer or having plunged it in to a snowdrift. The exaggeration is always extreme. I believe this is a left over of an arousal mechanism from early man who slept in dangerous conditions and could not afford to ignore surroundings, especially during sleep.

Recognising extrinsic stimuli

These dreams are usually easily spotted on waking. You just have to consider whether there is a stimulus that could have brought on the dream or set it going. There may be material in the dream that you want to look at, but it is usually fragmentary and of little significance.

I asked my patient whether he felt he wanted a sports car? Whether he had a problem with the car he drove? Whether he felt anxious in his dream? The answer to all these questions was "No". In fact, he mentioned his surprise that he had felt little pain or distress at having his arm wrenched off. He said that he had merely been interested to feel it go just before he woke. This was a dream that could be treated as purely from external stimulation. Even his feeling of mild distress at having his arm torn off gave him no pain within the dream and wore off at once when he found out the cause.

These dreams are very common, and reported frequently. If you are left with no strong feelings after you wake, and especially if you can trace the cause of the dream, and you often can, you have merely been wakened by some external source of sound, light or sensation. To become part of your dream, these stimuli must be strong enough to be noticed by your dreaming brain and yet not so acute that they waken you suddenly. They infiltrate your brain and become a part of the working dream process and eventually your brain says, "Well I can't do much with this," so over it goes to the waking mind and you wake up.

Noise

If you sleep on a noisy street you get used to the rattle of traffic and your dreams are unaffected by it, but a friend from the countryside coming to stay might dream of armies marching, or tanks sweeping across the desert, and would eventually waken to that dream and realise its cause. Your brain has accepted the noise as your normal night-time environment and will not waken you unless the character of the sound changes suddenly.

Light

During a holiday in France I remember dreaming that I was walking along the top of rolling hills. My holiday house was at the seaside so these hills were not local. They were more like the foothills of the Pentlands, which I know well from having lived in Edinburgh. The grass was short and springy and I had a companion with me who was a bit shadowy. I did not recognise her, but I was happy to have her with me. As we went along, tulip-shaped explosions burst out here and there, on the horizon, in the valley, over a little village that I could see in the distance.

"Don't worry about those," I said to my companion who seemed a bit alarmed. "They are just spontaneous combustions." We wandered on with these yellow explosions going off here and there until I began to hear the sound of cartwheels on a rutted road and looked round for the cause of this sound, and as I did I woke to the growl of thunder. I was in the middle of one of those spectacular sheet lightning storms that grumble away along the west coast of France. Interestingly, the shutters of my room were closed but had that heart-shaped hole in the middle that many French shutters do. The "spontaneous combustions" were the lightning flashes impinging on my retina, but maintaining the shape of the shutter hole. I wondered if my companion was in fact my more cowardly self because I am greatly afraid of lightning. I certainly went under the covers and hoped for the best, which is my usual response to these storms, but I knew where the dream came from.

Confusion of sounds

During another dream, I apparently woke to the doorbell ringing and I went downstairs to find the postman with a huge parcel. He said it was not for me, but it had my name on it, and I stood arguing with him until I suddenly realised I was just wearing my see-through nightie and standing in full view of both the postman and any passers-by. I then woke. It was quite muddling at first. I lay absolutely still and tried to come to my senses. As I did, I heard the tink tink tink of a blackbird just outside my window and the sound exactly mimicked the doorbell sound in my dream.

With a sigh I sadly abandoned the thought of a huge parcel and thankfully realised I had not been exposing myself, and became aware that it was becoming Spring again with the attendant escalation in birdsong.

Alarm clocks are often incorporated into dreams towards morning. I have heard all sorts of stories of people doing things from climbing Big Ben to being part of a police chase with whistles sounding in pursuit. Here is a more modern one.

A friend of mine is a writer and he had been doing quite a bit at his computer keyboard the day before. He dreamed that he was trying to get it to close down but it froze and, try as he would, the thing would not obey him. Instead, it started to bleep, on and on as if something frightful was happening. He woke much distressed to find it was just his alarm clock.

The pictures conjured up by these, often insignificant, external noises may be wild. A friend of mine described a dream where she was in the deep end of a swimming pool. "I had been collecting my daughter from her swimming lesson the afternoon before my dream," she explained. "I am always anxious that when she sees me she will turn and run down the side of the pool and will slip and her legs will go from under her and she will come down on her head. I constantly beg her to walk slowly by the poolside but she never does. I, myself, am a poor swimmer, so finding myself in the deep end of the pool was not a pleasure. I don't usually go there and even in my dream I was hanging on and looking round for my daughter. Suddenly a man plunged in head first beside me, went straight down to the bottom, and hit it with his head, 'Crump'. I heard the sound and he was dead. I knew that without anyone telling me. First 'Crump' and then he was dead. I woke at that moment and I thought, 'Where on earth did that dream come from?' "

"What did you feel about it?" I asked. "Nothing. I felt nothing. I did not know him. I never saw him before. There was just the noise of his head hitting the bottom and I woke knowing he was dead."

"Have you got noisy neighbours?", I asked. "Oh yes. We live in a tenement and the people in the flat up above are dreadful. Sometimes I think I am lucky to get to sleep at all."

My interpretation of that dream is that, whether or not she was about to go into a dream of anxiety about her fears for her daughter falling at the poolside, she was woken by the people upstairs dropping something heavy and this was incorporated in the last part of her dream as the sound woke her. When I suggested this to her she accepted it fully. She could not think why she had been so unaffected by an accident so close to her because she is a caring and kindly person. This was just the picture of a sound that woke her.

The significance of these dreams

These dreams are of no significance. You might say that her dream highlighted her fear of falls in the swimming pool area, as well as some anxiety on finding herself in the deep part of the pool. She might have wanted to allay these fears by taking swimming lessons herself and making sure her daughter didn't run at the poolside. The dream did not recur, so these anxieties were not deep ones, more likely the fleeting remembrance of unease from the previous afternoon, soon forgotten.

Internal stimuli

More important are the dreams that are set off by some stimulus within your body. Discomfort within your body may trigger dreams. One night I dreamed my leg became covered in black scabs. I was horrified and asked a passer by what it could be. ''Plague'', he said. ''It happens all the time in summer. It comes from the gardens you know.'' As I sorrowed over it I woke to find an itchy area at the back of one leg which, on investigation, obviously came from some creature in the long grass where I had been sitting on the previous warm summer evening. Plague it was not, nor was it serious, and application of a suitable salve removed its torment and any recurrence of the dream. It was an over reaction of my dreaming brain to some trivial internal stimulus.

I believe your body does often tell you quite early when things are not going right by infiltrating sensations into your dreams. These dream pictures are far more intense than the actual triggering stimulus. But the trigger is there, and should be looked at seriously. You would not have been warned by the dream unless your body felt that this was something foreign to it and of significance. Everyday aches and pains do not seem to figure in dreams unless they are suddenly becoming worse.

Pain

I recently cracked a rib. It was very foolish as I know my ribs fracture easily but I was putting a sleeping grandchild into her cot and my arms were not quite long enough to ground her gently and, as I leaned further over, she turned and I held her safe, but my weight on the cot side did the business. I felt the rib spring and knew I was in for three weeks of pain until healing occurred.

That night I dreamed I was at an Olympic Snooker Tournament. All at once the judges came to me and asked if I could adjudicate a match. ''But I don't know the rules,'' I excused myself. They paid no attention, merely pointing to a table and suggesting I learned how to do it. I found myself bent over the table, the rim digging in to my chest, and all the while asking pathetically if someone would show me the rules of the game so I would know how much to score for each shot.

It may have shown anxiety, but the place where the table was digging in to my ribs was exactly where the fracture was and when I woke I recognised the pain for what it was.

In the same way, you may dream that you are on a battlefield and some one has stuck a bayonet into your abdomen. You may not feel frightful agony, but you know it is serious and you are going to die. Waking, you find you are experiencing a mild colicky pain or perhaps an early bladder inflammation.

Paying attention to your body's signals

I believe these sorts of dreams usually herald trouble and are worth paying attention to. If the pain disappears you may forget it, but if a similar dream occurs on following nights, however slight the discomfort is on waking, I believe you should consider going along to your doctor to have it checked out. Repetitive dreams are significant and an interpretation should be attempted and acted on. Your body does tell you things in your dreams that you may discount by day or prefer not to notice.

I remember carrying my first baby. I had been a doctor on an obstetric ward and, at that time, was going to make my career in obstetrics, so I was reading books and examining patients very closely and had built up a fair amount of expertise. When I conceived I was delighted and expected a perfectly normal pregnancy as I could see no genetic or other problems. Gradually I became uneasy about the baby's progress. It was not one single thing, just a coming together of so many little targets not quite met. It was in the era of no ultrasound pictures so I depended on examination. The consultant was happy. My GP was happy. I was not. I felt my swelling abdomen for the baby's contours and I did not like what I felt. I spoke to the specialists and they laughed at me. Typical nervous doctor, I guess they thought. However I began dreaming that I had an anencephalic baby, where the head is not completcly formed and the baby is born dead. It wasn't a nice dream. I ignored it the first time. The second time, I again spoke to my GP but she told me firmly that the specialists were happy and I should just relax. In pregnancy one thinks silly things, she said, and of course she was right in that. By day I accepted her assumptions. By night I dreamed I had an anencephalic baby.

Of course I was right. I wished I had not been. It took months before the specialists also became unhappy about my progress. I was a specialist. I knew what I was feeling. My dreams told me the truth when my daytime self was able to shrug off my findings and believe my doctors.

Later, much later, I realised that I had probably had German measles at the time when I conceived. Again, at that time doctors did not know of the foetal dangers inherent with that disease. I never thought about it at the time. Nowadays, I would have been a great deal more careful. You get over these things and once you have your big lovely family the grieving does not hurt you any more. It is the luck of the draw and has made me perhaps a more caring doctor. I hope so. But my dreams of that baby did not recur once I had a definite diagnosis, nor thereafter. This was not a casual dream. It was an interpretation of what was going on in my body, as assessed by an expert in the field. If I ever met a similar case I would make very sure that the dreams had no pointers before I dismissed such a vivid recurring dream as a nervous reaction to an unknown situation.

Diseases

There are many diseases, from cancer to stomach ulcers, where a dream begins the process of unease that eventually takes a person to his or her doctor. In your waking state you put off going to see about a problem. It seems too small, too insignificant, and you are a busy person with no time to waste at the doctor's. But, by night, the problem receives a more sympathetic appraisal by your dreaming brain and the half anxieties, stifled by day, surface to focus on what your inner self sees as a real problem.

These are not dreams of prognostication. You are not being visited by divine powers, or indeed any sort of power. You are sensing, in your dream, the first and minimal stimulus of something that is not quite right, usually long before you accept you have a problem by day. The magnification of tiny feelings that occur in dreamtime is alerting you to the fact that all is not well. An occasional dream of something wrong here or there is not significant. It is likely that we feel the odd inconsequential pain in sleep, just as we do by day. If the dream is repetitive, coming in different forms maybe, but always pinpointing the same place, then that is significant and deserves your close attention. If you cannot be absolutely sure what the dream is telling you then you should visit your doctor who is trained to find out and will be delighted to be offered something in its early stages to diagnose because treatment is usually so much easier.

For instance, I spotted a rodent ulcer – a pre-cancerous lesion, which usually starts at the prenatal skin joins of the face – at the inner corner of a young man's eyebrow. "When did that start?" I asked. "I've had it some time," he confessed. "I kept hoping it would go away but it hasn't. It seems to be getting bigger. The funny thing is I started dreaming about it. First I had a bird on my head pecking me there, then I had a huge blister that seemed to bulge out before me, and, though no one noticed as I walked along, I felt like a freak."

"You should have come to see me when you started dreaming about it," I told him. "But you are in plenty of time now. It is very early and I will have it zapped in no time." He never did have a recurrence but his story convinced me that our bodies do use dreams as early warning systems.

Menstruation

Repetitive dreams do not usually come from normal body functions. For instance, dreams occurring about menstrual time are usually of a sexual nature, and dysmenorrhoea, the pain associated with menstruation, is not usually magnified unless it is very severe. I did have quite painful periods at one time and on occasion I can remember dreaming of suddenly starting labour pains and in my dream becoming aware that I was about to deliver a baby, only to wake, thinking, ''Bother, another period, and a sore one.'' But this was never repetitive. It was merely an occasional assessment of the appearance of an unusual pain that could be cured.

If you are worried that you are not going to get a period, then around the time when one is due you may well get anxiety dreams where you feel threatened or frightened. That is not the same mechanism. That is an assessment by your dreaming mind of what you have been doing to put yourself at risk of pregnancy or, in later years perhaps, your fear of the menopause. In both of these situations, if your dreams are repetitive you need expert help. Your mind is telling you that you need professional counselling at the least, if not medical advice. These dreams do not trouble you if the pregnancy is wanted or the menopause is accepted as a natural and non-threatening event.

Women who want to become pregnant may at the same time feel nervous about the whole idea and then may experience anxiety dreams. These dreams are easily prevented by talking the worries through with the doctor who is caring for them through their pregnancy.

Typical intrinsic signal dreams

There are some very typical dreams that are attached to different body systems and if you have them you should talk to your doctor about them.

The heart

People who have heart problems do seem to dream dreams of physical labour. It is as if, when the pump that keeps your circulation going is faulty, you not only feel tired by day, you dream that you are exhausted by night. Struggling along a long road with a weight on your back is a typical dream. Your arms and legs are leaden. There may be a touch of anxiety about the dream as well, so that although you can scarcely lift one foot after another you feel that there is something after you. These are not real nightmares, though they can become so. In these, the dream material is florid, the pictures spacious and wild. Increasing heart failure often shows itself at night by a feeling of breathlessness in your dream. In your dream, you are at the end of your tether, carrying a sack of potatoes on your back or toiling up the last mile in a marathon. The road appears endless and you are dry and panting.

I experienced just this sort of dream one holiday in Tibet. It had been a long-time ambition of mine to go there and the experience was truly amazing and has left me with life-long pictures of sheer beauty. However, on stepping from the plane at 12,000 feet it did not take me long at all to get mountain sickness, and during the worst moments I needed oxygen. I might have retreated without ever seeing the place, but the planes then stopped coming as climatic conditions were unsuitable for landing and take off. We were left marooned in the hotel with the benefits of Tibetan medicine, which is well aware of mountain sickness, and amazing rubber pillows filled with oxygen, which were deposited by my bedside with kind regularity. There was nothing to do but rest and get better or worse and take the medication I had luckily brought with me for just this sort of occurrence.

By day I was as comfortable as repeated vomiting and extreme weakness allowed me to be. By night, my dreams were horrendous. Every night in my dreams I walked ceaselessly. On one night, it was over the yellow stony waste of foothills that I could see from my hotel room. I stumbled along with the bright sun blazing down from a blue clear sky. I was tired, so tired, and my legs were like rubber but I had to go on or die and I knew it. There was a weight on my back. I must have been carrying something but I didn't know what. I could not get rid of it. I just plodded on and on apparently all night. I was thankful to wake from that dream in the morning. The day, by contrast, seemed a better time. I had more freewill to help myself.

These dreams continued every night until I began to get better. Once I was up and about they stopped and did not return. I was in no doubt what they were telling me and the fact that they did stop confirmed my feeling that there was no permanent damage.

Blood pressure

Increasing or high blood pressure tends to make you dream aggressive dreams of fighting or arguing with people in an uncontrolled way that you would be unlikely to do in normal life. Someone does something that displeases you in your dream and you fly off the handle and harangue them at length, waking exhausted by your fury, and often with your teeth gritted against a headache that improves when you get up.

Again, a single dream is not diagnostic. It is when this sort of dream becomes a feature of your night-time dreaming that you should look at it seriously and do something about it.

You always have to bear in mind that some medicines used to treat high blood pressure cause dreaming in their own right. Most notable in this field are the beta-blockers where the wider spectrum drugs such as propranolol may stimulate wild and distressing dreams if not true nightmares. You should always bear this in mind if you start treatment for this or indeed any other condition and your dreams change and become hard to tolerate. Your doctor can change your prescription to a medication that will allow you peaceful sleep. There is no point in going from one set of bad symptoms to another.

The lungs

Any condition that affects your lungs, and therefore interferes with the oxygen supply to your brain, has an effect on your dreaming. In REM sleep the circulation to the brain is greatly increased. The brain is obviously searching for and requiring an increased supply of blood borne nutrients to do the job it needs to do before morning to set your brain ready for the strains you will put on it all day.

You have also to remember that in REM sleep your muscles lie flaccid, all except your diaphragm which continues to keep your breathing going. However, in REM sleep the ancillary muscles of your chest are not involved so those people who routinely use these muscles to assist their breathing process are not getting the help they are used to by day, when they are in dream sleep.

Asthmatics and those people who suffer from chronic bronchitis are used to this and take medication to assist their lung function by night. However, the first sign that they may have an infection starting, with its effect of worsening the lung function, or indeed any worsening of function, is often pinpointed by a change in normal dreaming to dreams of running races or hurrying for trains; in fact, always being late and breathless. These dreams may also have touches of anxiety in that the dreamer may feel pursued, but the main feeling is one of breathlessness and I believe it is a significant finding and one that, if repeated, should be further investigated as soon as possible, even if by day there is no obvious reason for it.

Serious snorers sometimes go on to that condition called Obstructive Sleep Apnoea where, because your soft palate falls back to block your throat periodically, your inhalation is limited and you begin to suffer from a chronic lack of oxygen in the brain, as well as other organs.

Your brain in REM sleep demands extra oxygen and gets it with the increase of circulation that occurs. However, if that is not occurring you tend to suffer from anxiety type dreams. You find yourself running away from a Tyrannosaurus Rex through a tangle of jungle plants. You feel breathless and frightened and you may in fact go on to suffer repetitive nightmares. Your brain does not put up with even minimal oxygen lack and lets you know about it in your dreams. So if you know you snore loudly and then your dreams suddenly change for the worse it is worth checking with your doctor that you don't need treatment for the condition. There are sleep laboratories in most big towns these days and Obstructive Sleep Apnoea can be diagnosed very easily and treated equally efficiently. You do not need to suffer bad dreams if you listen to what they are telling you.

The stomach

Dreams of being stabbed in the stomach may herald gastric ulcer pain, even though when you wake after this dreadful experience, you find that the pain is quite minimal. If the dream recurs it is worth having it checked out. Anyone may wake after an unaccustomed and heavy meal having dreamed that they were in a tiny sailing ship out at the mercy of huge waves and, as they go up and down, feeling more and more queasy, they are thrown on to an anchor, carelessly left on deck, and feel the barb sink into their abdomen, to wake crying out for help and feeling distinctly nauseated with the pain of indigestion. There is no problem in tracing the dream to the symptoms and their cause. It only needs a trip to the medicine cupboard for a stomach settler and a vow not to over indulge again. However, repetitive dreaming where you wake after some sort of abdominal accident and notice that you do have discomfort in that position is, I believe, a cause for concern and requires some sort of effort to find the cause.

Distinguishing between physical signals and anxiety dreams

You do need to be able to distinguish between these dreams where you are left with a real pain, and those where, while they appear similar, they are really just dreams borne out of strong feelings through the previous day.

A patient who knew I was interested in dreams told me that he had dreamed that he had swallowed his cigarette lighter. I wondered if he was feeling the early symptoms of some throat condition and asked him about this.

"No", he said. "There was no feeling of stretching. There was no pain as it went down. I was quite surprised to feel it go down so easily." "What else did you feel?" "My main feeling was of how silly I had been to put it in a position where it could be swallowed. I wished I had not done it and I said to myself, 'Oh dear. Now that is going to cause some bother later on.' "

I felt he had done or said something, either at work or at home that he was seriously regretting and was aware that he should not have done. His feelings at the end of the dream suggested that he was going to have to do something to rectify the situation. When I told him this he looked both guilty and relieved. "I was afraid it was something in my throat," he said. "I'm glad it is not."

He did not dream about his throat again, but I had it fully investigated because of his anxiety and was able to reassure him totally on that score. He later confessed that, while he was glad to be clear of the anxiety of throat cancer (which is what he had been afraid of), he had a very good idea of what he had done to cause that dream. It had been a dream of feelings, not a dream caused by an internal stimulus, though the fact that he was a smoker was obviously causing him some anxiety.

Prophetic dreams

Everyone knows someone who says that they have had a prophetic dream. I do not hold to the belief that these dreams come from a divine source. I believe they are a mixture of dream material from extrinsic and intrinsic sources and are very accurate assessments made without the overlay of the many different opinions which colour your everyday thoughts.

By day, you may ignore small aches and pains or occurrences at work, or in the home situation, only to have them highlighted in a dream. Your brain has cleared all the trivialities and wishful thinking of the day and the real problems are left.

If you dream that you are out at a party and your nearest and dearest is dancing with someone else, and when you ask him or her why he is doing that he or she says, ''Well, it gets boring at home, doesn't it? I need some light frivolity. I find this person more fun than you'', you may wake feeling upset and afraid that you are no longer the favoured partner. Perhaps, then, it is time to look at your relationship more closely. Are you giving your partner the right amount of loving attention? Are you expecting him or her to tag along while you jet set about? Are you ignoring a relationship you value, expecting it to thrive on very little attention, while you pursue other interests? All relationships need fertilising with love and they do founder, often unnecessarily, because you have so much to do in your life that you are busy, busy, busy, and ignore the needs of your partner. Your dreams, however, pick up on your real feelings and can show you when you are at risk of alienating your partner by ignoring his or her needs. In the same way, your dreams will pick up a cooling of love and attention from a partner far sooner than your day time senses will allow. If your dreams are repetitive you should consider watching for signs of infidelity and certainly be looking to get your relationship back to the way it was when you were not dreaming these dreams.

Many people will tell you of friends who have escaped death because they dreamed of a bomb explosion the night before they were due to go on a certain outing, and so called it off; or perhaps people who dreamed of being in a road accident and so refused to go on a bus tour where, indeed, the bus did hit something.

There has to be some possibility of coincidence here, though it could be that your more focused dreaming brain may anticipate trouble that your daytime confidence does not allow.

A young lady told me that she had been asked to a party by some of her university friends. She admitted that she did not know them very well and she was not too comfortable about where the party was being held, but the night before the party she dreamed that she was in a basement looking for her particular friend when an earthquake struck. She was struggling to get out, with ruins all about her, when she woke.

She did not think much about this at the time, but when someone got a chip pan fire going at the party and they all had to rush outside she thought she had had a prophetic dream and would, I know, tell people about it for ever afterwards.

In fact, she did accept that she was uneasy about going to the party. Her particular friend said he was probably not going to be there. He did not care for the people who neither of them knew well, except for one girl who was in her class and had begged her to come as company for her. I saw the dream as a perfectly normal anxiety dream highlighting her unease at being stuck in a basement with a lot of people she did not like and who might be doing things like drugs and drinking to excess, which she didn't approve of. That the cooker went on fire merely confirmed a sensible assessment of the sort of party where disaster is very likely, and the sort of invitation that she should not have accepted. She would, however, always feel she had had a divine warning.

Acting upon your dreams

Your dreams may seem bizarre, but if you interpret them correctly you will be aware of their meaning in your own mind. It is often better to do something earlier about your dreams than waiting till they come true.

For instance, if you dream that you have lost your children and are searching for them through a school where no one seems to have seen them, and the teachers who you know should have taught them refuse to admit any knowledge of them, you may certainly accept that this is a dream of anxiety.

With your children so firmly in the starring part it is quite possible that you are anxious about one or other of them. It may just be that you are allowing them to travel home from school by themselves for the first time and you are anxious for them and worried about what you would do if they did not show up on time. It may be that you sense that you are no longer in their confidence and that they are being secretive in a way that, by day, you had scarcely noticed, but your dream is showing you. You will know whether this sort of dream (which is very common to mothers) means that you are just a little anxious about allowing your children more self regulation and freedom, or whether you have begun to notice odd differences in their behaviour that should alert you to look more closely at what they are doing after school. It may also be the case that, if you are working, you are beginning to feel that you need more time with your children, that you need to adjust your hours so that you may be together more often, so that you can participate in their education and lives more fully.

No analyst can tell you as precisely what your dreams mean as you can. They can only encourage you to do something about what your dreams are showing you.

Have you ever dreamed about being left on your own to struggle with some Herculean task, either mountains of filing at the office or piles of ironing at home? Is this prophetic or is it beginning to happen in real life? It is most likely that if the dream recurs you are beginning to experience that feeling of hopeless struggle in some aspect of your life and you should do something about it before it all becomes too much for you.

Toilet dreams

No chapter on intrinsic stimuli would be complete without mention of dreams of wandering along looking for a place to pass urine only eventually to wake needing the toilet. You are, by education, shy of passing urine in public. So, in your dream, when you feel the need to urinate, sometimes you are too deeply asleep to wake to the first physical prompt and you incorporate the desire to urinate in your dream. However, you have also the inbuilt teaching not to urinate in your bed, so your brain knows you cannot just pass water. It gives you a miserable dream of searching for somewhere suitable.

Here is one such dream: "I was staying at a sort of small hotel or bed and breakfast establishment that had no en-suite toilet. I knew they were all down the corridor so I set off in my nightie. The nearest one was occupied and there was a nasty-looking, middle-aged blonde in a trench coat hovering around the door so I went on. The corridors twisted and turned and there were no other toilets. I was getting desperate and wondered if I could use a large plant pot that was sat in one corner. As I approached it a man opened a door and peered at me suspiciously. I was mortified because he seemed to know what I was contemplating. I hurried on, and now I was in a three dimensional maze that had little stairs every few yards, and I wanted to squat in a corner but knew it would start a river flowing down the stairs if I did and then everyone would know that I had done this anti-social thing. I went on further and at last there was a toilet with its door open. I went in but others pushed in with me and I woke, feeling the need to urinate."

Another dream, from a man this time: "I was in a gents'

toilet, but a very ornamental one. The urinal was done in extremely ornate Victorian ironwork and painted in two shades of blue and looked like a sort of window seat with swags and tassels. In order to stop people from accidentally sitting down on it instead of urinating in it there was a fence around it, which still allowed it to be used but you had to pee from a distance and be extremely accurate. I was just lining up to do so when I woke.''

I have had dreams of actually managing to urinate and waking to a feeling of relief that changes to horror on waking in case I have wet the bed. I have never done so and I believe that what is happening in my dream is that the bladder contracts, causing the feeling of urgent need and then partially relaxes for a while and this feeling is sometimes translated by the dreaming brain into actual urination. Not wetting the bed must be a powerfully trained body function because I have never wet the bed in these dreams.

However, it is not always so for all people and I have had dream reports from patients who do manage to relieve themselves in their dream and wake to a wet bed. They are, in the main, those who are on sedative or relaxant medication. Sometimes those who have heavily overindulged in alcohol experience the same unfortunate occurrence. Those whose bedtime control of the bladder is weak also may have these dreams of needing to urinate and wake having urinated. Usually, however, they are simple intrinsic stimuli dreams that tell you that you need to pass water on waking.

Dreams of defecation are less common. This one was reported to me by a patient who had had an episode of loose stools: ''It was our wedding day and I was getting ready for the ceremony at a large hotel. I needed to defecate and, as I thought the groom shouldn't have something like that on his mind at this special occasion, I went into a toilet, although I was aware I would have to hurry as time was going on. The lavatory itself was a thing like a small electronic weighing scale in the middle of the floor. I was disconcerted to find that there were large and completely transparent windows along one wall, and that the bathroom was overlooked by several other windows in the same building. I moved back against the wall for greater privacy, but this seemed to make things worse. Somehow the bathroom was now in the open air; also, I knew that unless I hurried I would be late for my wedding. I moved again, this time into a trench on the other side of a small ridge; however, this was overlooked by students' quarters. The students didn't seem to take much interest, but unfortunately I now discovered that the trench was also occupied by several tourists, some of them actually eating sandwiches. I was just about to struggle out of the trench to find somewhere else when I woke, needing to go to the bathroom to defecate.''

All these dreams of a natural process, whose performance is governed by social regulations taught in childhood, are dreams where your socially aware brain is being chivvied by the natural impulse. Rather than an immediate wakening, your working brain in dream sleep is brought to realise that you need to urinate or defecate, but has overall control still in place that prevents you doing so in bed. Primitive man may not have had these dreams. There is always an element of anxiety about these dreams, but I believe it is mostly the anxiety associated with not wanting to act against the custom learned in childhood of remaining clean in bed.

8

DREAMS OF DEPRIVATION, INCLUDING SEXUAL DEPRIVATION

Dreams of sex

When I talked about writing a book on dreams the first reaction I got was, "How interesting. You know, if I haven't had sex for a while I dream of it."

Some people don't like to speak about dreams of intercourse and many people don't even want to think of them in case it shows that they have abnormal mental activity. But dreams of sex are very normal and are usually dreams of deprivation. Psychologists suggest that your sexual urge is one of the strongest in your make up. Unsatisfied, it surfaces in your dreams at night, though by day you are too taken up with your job or family to have time to desire sex.

By day, your adrenaline is running and sex is put on the back burner. By night, when you are relaxed, your brain reminds you of the natural urges that are normal to humans, and if you have not had intercourse for some time your dreams may be pretty wild ones.

Adolescent sexual dreams

For those who have never had intercourse, dreams of sexual deprivation are often those of yearning. I believe some dreams of flying, where you are swooping about in marvellous attire, showing off in front of an admiring audience or cuddling comfortable objects, may be early sexual dreams.

Boys learn about masturbation and intercourse at an early age. My male colleagues assure me that, by adolescence, boys are perambulating penises; their waking moments full of fantasy or hope of sexual encounter, their night-time dreams full of wild experiences, leading to intercourse and orgasm. ''Wet'' dreams are very much a normal part of male adolescence.

Men's sexual dreams

Men normally have an erection in REM sleep. It is clear that sexual desire is a strong male motivator and, if a man does not satisfy his sexual urges by day, he may well wake to a remembered erotic dream.

Sex with people other than your spouse

Even if sexually satisfied, men have dreams of arousal. I have heard dream reports from happily married men of exotic women from the previous night's television viewing, or particularly attractive friends from work, or their wife's social group appearing in their bedrooms and running their nails over their thighs, cuddling up beside them in bed or dancing with them so close that they can feel their bodies all the way up.

There is no need to feel anxious or guilty about these dreams. They are merely coloured pictures to illustrate your feelings. You may find yourself having sex with animals, sons, daughters, casual acquaintances or even the Wife of Bath if you were reading Chaucer's *Canterbury Tales* the night before.

Whom you have sex with in your dreams is of no significance, so long as when you wake you are aware that your dream was merely illustrating a feeling, that you have no desire actually to repeat the occasion for real and that in some of the cases, the idea is completely unacceptable and would disgust you very much.

Perversion

I have no expert knowledge of the dreams of sexual perverts. My guess is that, if they dream of their perversion, they wake to want it, or at least they have no strong feelings of conscience that provide the normal feeling of being offended for having produced such an unwanted dream.

You cannot control what your dream shows you. You can look at it in the light of day and find it offensive, but use the feeling from it to tell you that perhaps you are seeking more love or sex, and search for that in an acceptable context instead.

I do not believe that your dreams are trying to turn you into a pervert. I believe that when your dreaming brain is searching after material to colour a picture of sexual deprivation, it looks for strong feelings of desire and picks them up from a filing system that is not one we would naturally use. It may be that your short term memories of a recent dinner with an exotic friend have been laid down beside your current sexual need, and so, when the one feeling is triggered, the brain uses the nearest available, material to colour its feeling with a picture. It does not mean that you love your partner less or that you lust after someone else's to any degree. Though, of course, it might do. Only you can tell the real meaning, the essential feeling that has been shown you.

One word of warning: if you are not affected by guilt or shame following a violent, abnormal or seriously antisocial dream involving sex, and in the day time you begin to fancy repetition of that act, knowing it to be illegal or seriously against normal social or religious views, you should seek help and advice from a doctor. Perversion may show itself first in your dreams and is more readily cured before it becomes an actuality.

Unusual sex

One of my patients reported a dream of having had loving intercourse with her cat. ''Of course it was ridiculous,'' she explained. ''My cat must have increased in size considerably to make it possible. I felt his warm cuddly black fur all round me and it was very pleasant.''

''What happened when you woke?'' I asked. ''Well, of course I felt pretty stupid because it was such a ridiculous dream and I knew where it came from. My cat was in my bed doing his best to push me out so I just vacated, got into my husband's bed, and he was delighted to find me all excited and we had excellent sex. I then put the cat back in his bed where he should have been put last thing that evening, tucked myself up in my own bed and finished the night satisfied and dreamlessly.''

Her husband is a large dark haired man so her dream may have had some of its origin in that fact too. Your dream filing system is not similar to your waking office system.

Women's sexual dreams

Women's sexual dreams may be just as erotic as those of their male counterparts but do often have a considerable amount of cuddling and warmth, loving and caring. Perhaps this reflects their greater desire towards achieving security in a sexual relationship. This naturally varies both from woman to woman, and indeed from man to man, as well as altering as sexual experience is gained. There is no blueprint for sexual dreams through life.

Guilt

Very often you wake to an immense sense of guilt and revulsion as you review your dream material. You certainly don't want to tell that dream to your nearest and dearest, though on occasion to tell your friends at work that you dreamed you 'had it off' with some sex symbol or other is an act of bravado that provokes catcalls and half envious teasing.

Your guilt is brought on by knowing that, in your dream, you have broken a rule that you have been educated to respect. If you had no such training and indoctrination you would not feel guilt about any of your acts. Society would be in mayhem. Even animals have inbuilt rules of conduct. In humans these have been laid down over centuries in sophisticated legal and religious systems where punishments or social ostracism threaten those who break the regimen of the accepted code of behaviour.

So if you wake, having dreamed of having had warm and loving intercourse with a near relation, your first morning thought is, "What a disgusting thing to have thought of doing." I do not believe that your brain is trying to show you the joys of an incestuous relationship. It is merely that your body is missing the delights of sexual intercourse and, in giving you that message, it may use anybody that you love, or anybody whom you have seen and admired. It is seeking to show you the type of sexual involvement you are looking for, perhaps something more exciting, more caring or more exotic. The hints are there so look for them. Don't turn away from the dream with revulsion.

Say to yourself, "Now, that was completely out of line. I am revolted by the whole idea of, say, having sex with my mother, but is it that I am looking for someone with her welcoming warm love, who would be there for me only? Is my dream using my mother, but meaning someone who gives me those feelings, who I haven't seen for some time, so is not immediately available to my dream material file? I saw my mother yesterday and I felt I could really talk to her, just as I did to Miss X, now that I remember her. Perhaps I am beginning to want to settle down and have a more lasting relationship with someone who I can really talk to.''

Analysing sexual dreams

Again, only you will know what the dream really means. What you can be pretty clear on is that the feeling is not as simple as the dream. Unlike Freud, I believe you are unlikely to be actually wanting to have sex with your mother. If you are, the dream is perhaps a warning that it is time you matured and looked for the same qualities in someone your own age. Your REM brain is not matchmaking; it is simply trying to create a picture of deprivation.

After you have got over the shock and horror of having intercourse with someone or something that is totally unacceptable, look further into the dream, ignoring the actual love object, but concentrating on the feelings you felt with them. Because the sex urge is a strong one it attracts other strong desires to it. Look, therefore, past the act of intercourse to what you felt at the time. Did you have a desire to be held and comforted? Did you wish to show off and be admired? You may accept the simple message that your body is missing sex. That may or may not be easily remedied. Having sex with your partner will stop dreams of sexual intercourse repeating but remembering the feelings your dream engendered may allow you to improve your relationship or encourage variety in your love making.

These days, having sex with just anyone is dangerous at best, and may be life threatening, as there are incurable sexually transmitted diseases which may prove fatal. Masturbation to orgasm is just as effective in alleviating sexual deprivation. You won't get AIDS from your hands.

It is more important to understand the desires that went with your dream. Did you feel young, strong and beautiful and want to be noticed? Does that mean that you feel unappreciated at home or in the office? You can do something about that. Relationships may be improved by understanding. Talking things out may help.

Did you dream of having sex with your boss? You don't need to, to improve his opinion of your work! Your dream was probably telling you that, on the one hand, you were missing sex and, on the other, that you felt your boss did not appreciate you sufficiently. There are two separate feelings amalgamated here in one dream. Of course, your dream might be telling you that you fancied your boss rotten! You are the best person to know which is the true meaning.

Did you feel safe and warmly loved in your dream? Did you enjoy long dalliance beforehand? Could you make these things better with your real life partner? Your dream may be suggesting you would be more content if you do.

Mediaeval herbals are full of recipes to prevent ''dreams of lechery''. Herbalists of that time were well aware that the sexual urge was one of the strongest in your physical make up and tended to surface in dreams when physical satisfaction of it was denied. Having said that, they did not go on to suggest that the feelings included in your dream deprivation package are likely to be just as important and possibly easier to do something about.

Your dream's sexual partner

Interestingly, you seldom seem to have intercourse with your own partner in dreams if he or she is readily available. That would be wholly acceptable and very agreeable. I believe that this is because, if you do have intercourse before you sleep, you are not deprived so you don't dream about having sex; and if you have not had intercourse for a while, your brain in REM sleep gives you pictures of sexual deprivation, but adds in any other strong feelings it can't mitigate and file in memory so the dream picture material is never simple.

For instance, if you lack assurance, your dream might be of being cuddled by something big and strong and comforting, as likely to be a bear as a person. On the other hand, if you are simply sexually deprived, you may dream of intercourse with a television character viewed the night before and have little added feeling, just the satisfaction of the act itself.

It may be that, if you have recently lost a partner, you will find yourself having sex with him or her. Your dream may be comforting or bizarre. The two motivational forces acting in your dream are your own sexual deprivation coupled with your feelings of, perhaps, loss, anxiety or anger at being abandoned or left in need of comfort. Accept that sort of dream as part of a grieving and healing process.

Acting on sexual dreams

Husbands and wives in the hurly-burly of family life have dreams of sexual deprivation. Again, the feelings that come with the dream may show where unsatisfied needs have built up. Are you looking for more interest in yourself, more loving attention? These things communicated by day can enrich a relationship that has become humdrum. Did you feel warm, loved and cared for? Is this something you miss in your daytime life? Can you do something about it?

If you are lonely, can you join a group of people with like interests? If your sex is not satisfying, can you encourage your partner to enjoy it more in a way that gives you that loved and cared for feeling? If you are young and entering a relationship, is the dream highlighting a lack of loving that you are unwilling to acknowledge or hope will improve with time? Make sure it does before you finalise the relationship for life.

Because it is sometimes embarrassing to talk to anyone about these sexual dreams, it is sensible to be able to interpret them yourself. They are usually very obvious once you have got over any guilt and shock following the event.

If there is no guilt, because yours was an unattached person's dream of sex with a beautiful partner, look carefully at the person of your dreams. Notice the parts about them that you like best: their manner, their build and colouring, the feelings they engender in you. It may tell you a great deal about the sort of ideal mate you are looking for. This may or may not be the person you later form a loving relationship with, as you must realise that body form is not the first requisite for long-term happiness. It is, however, a type, be it tall and dark or short and red haired, that you have a natural preference for and may keep as your 'pin up' for life. If your lasting relationship is a good one, there will almost certainly be something of that man or woman of your dreams in your partner.

People prone to sexual dreams

If you are celibate through religious decision or from lack of an available partner you will be prone to dreams of intercourse. Women are more likely to have them towards and during menstruation when their vaginal area is engorged and more sensitive, also at mid-cycle when they are ovulating. Men have no such cyclical increase in dream libido, but thoughts of sex the previous day or explicit or erotic pictures seen on television often precipitate sexual dreams. Usually both men and women wake to orgasm, even if the woman seldom gets an orgasm at intercourse.

Menopausal and postmenopausal women do not stop having sexual dreams. Young partners are often dreamed of and there is usually a strong need to be cosseted and loved, shown in the dream material as well as active sexual action. If you are having this sort of dream repeatedly, masturbation to orgasm or increased intercourse with your partner will almost certainly reduce their frequency. Otherwise, accept them as occasional comfort to your sexual nature. If you need to seek pardon for it, do so, but you are merely human and, although human urges may be well sublimated by day, dreams are not under the control of your waking mind.

In the main, a dream of intercourse that you have enjoyed

should be accepted as a loving experience whose feelings could be transferred into your own, more socially appropriate, day time relationships to make your sex act more satisfying and your relationship more fulfilling.

Other forms of deprivation

Sexual deprivation is just one body lack that is highlighted in dreams. There are a host of deprivation dreams and they are not hard to interpret.

Cigarettes

About sixty per cent of ex-smokers have dreams of enjoying a cigarette. They usually wake, horrified to think that they are still smoking, and are thankful on waking to find it a dream.

One ex-smoker said to me, "I dreamed I was only smoking five a day and kept telling myself that the statistics of lung cancer could not apply to me. When I woke I was so thankful to realise that I had not smoked for two years."

These dreams become less frequent the longer you are from smoking cessation. They may be prevented by using nicotine patches or chewing nicotine gum but are seldom such a serious problem that you need to resort to these steps once you have stopped completely and need no day time aids to keep you abstinent.

I did once attempt to smoke a cigarette. It gave me no pleasure and I have never done so since and I have never smoked in a dream. Non-smokers seem not to. This is a pure dream of deprivation where the body still misses in dreams what you have decided against by day.

Alcohol

Abstaining alcoholics experience the same sort of dream where they find themselves in a pub and once more enjoy the feeling of quantities of beer flowing over their throats, with the following sensation of well being and loss of anxiety.

Going over the reasons why you stopped taking alcohol and reinforcing the positive benefits of abstinence is a useful procedure following one of these dreams. If they become very obtrusive you should talk to your doctor about them. He can give you a short course of medication to suppress dreaming and break the cycle of repetitive temptation by night. It then may not recur.

Food

If you are slimming, hunger finds its way into your dreams. I remember, during one of my efforts to lose a little weight after Christmas overeating, I dreamed I was in a pastry shop. Before me under glass were the most marvellous looking cake slices, sponges, iced confections. It was a mouth-watering sight. I chose a pastry sandwich filled with cream and covered in icing. The shop lady passed it over on a little piece of greaseproof paper and I took it, opened my mouth and took one delicious bite, waking to find my mouth full of duvet.

''Poor old body mechanism'', I thought. It might have been trying to tell me something, but my need to regain a correct working weight was more important to me. The dreams would just have to be my only pleasure on the eating front!

Drink

Similarly, thirst produces dreams such as pursuing water heard trickling in a desert. Water is deeply necessary to your body. Your brain in sleep makes every effort to show your need for water if you become deprived of it. Thirst is a strong body feeling and is rapidly shown in REM sleep. I suspect that, where continual thirst and urination is one of the first symptoms of disease, as it is in diabetes, the symptoms are highlighted in dream sleep almost before the body is aware of the problem by day.

In fever you often dream of looking for water to drink and it does appear that if you manage to find a long cool drink and enjoy it in your dream you are not as desperate for liquid as if you never reach the water you are searching for.

Bereavement

Deprivation dreams following the death or absence of a loved one show more commonly as anxiety dreams or dreams of pursuing something or someone that you badly want. The death of someone near to you may cause you to have nightmares as your own inborn fear of death is suddenly brought to prominence in your thoughts. Medication suppressing REM sleep and encouraging a full night's oblivion may be appropriate for a short time to give you space to push through the various stages of grief and mourning, the loss, the anger at being left, the guilt at being the survivor, the worry about how you are going to go on alone; especially if these thoughts are causing nightmares.

As your grief becomes less acute you may have reflective dreams where you meet and talk to the friends or relations that you love and have lost. Sometimes you are unaware that they are dead or gone away. It does not occasion any surprise or comment. You wake and may feel an acute pang of loss, but usually your dream is a comforting one. Your loved one has said something useful or offered advice on a current problem. What appears to be happening is that you are sorting out a problem in your own mind and you have used the covering material of the person you have loved to produce your answer. Often it is just the sort of answer they would have given.

One dream report I got was from a young woman who had just been left by her long-term boyfriend and was grieving dreadfully for him. She came to me first because she was having nightmares which had a clear base in the anxiety of being left on her own for the first time in her life as her boyfriend had been a school chum before they moved in together. Luckily, she got a promotion in her work soon after. It may not have been coincidental because she found relief in working late and going home tired. She came to tell me of her new job, which would entail travelling a good deal and meeting new people. "I dreamed Alan and I were walking on Salisbury Crags, just as we used to on summer evenings. He was just as usual and I told him I was going into a new sort of life and do you know what he said, Doctor?"

I shook my head.

"He said, 'You'll do it very well and the people will be just as grown up as you are.' When I woke I missed him but he seemed further away and I did not need him as badly any more." She appeared to have found peace of mind.

Dreams following loss very often replace that loss. A friend of mine whose much-loved cat died dreamed that the animal suddenly appeared and was sniffing at his foot. Overjoyed he called his wife to come and see that their cat had returned but she did not answer him and then he had the feeling that in fact she would not be able to see the animal even if she had come. He sat and feasted his eyes on his much loved cat, afraid to move lest it disappear. In fact it seemed to come and go several times in the dream, always bringing a feeling of delight when it reappeared. He told me he had several dreams where his cat was doing the normal things he used to and then the dream would become bizarre and end.

The loss of any deep love is as strong an emotion as sex and will show in your dreams until you have managed to achieve peace of mind about the loss, either by sublimation, such as getting a new kitten, beginning a new relationship, locking the hurting memories away or bringing them into your normal living.

After-death sightings
Dreams where you see your loved ones are not the same as the occasionally reported after-death sightings of a loved one, usually a husband or wife. These phenomena are seldom discussed because the person to whom they occur is overwhelmed by them and often suspicious that he is hallucinating and going 'off his head'. They break all codes of everyday life but are documented in medical journals.

I had a patient once, an old lady, whose husband had just died. I had attended him and got to know them both very well, which was why she eventually burst out with the information that her husband had come back to see her.

"I think I am going mad," she said. "I saw my husband last night. It was not a dream. He came and sat on my bed for a chat, just as he always did before we turned in."

"What did you talk about?" I asked. "Just little things," she said. "He told me it wasn't bad being dead. I was half afraid, half happy to see him."

"How do you feel now?" "Comforted," she said.

Comfort is the usual feeling gained from these after-death experiences. They seem to happen towards evening, or when the couple would normally be alone together. They are not dreams. They have never been explained in medical literature, just documented. It is usually enough to reassure the person having them that they are not demented or going mad and that this is a known happening that usually gets less frequent and stops with time. The episodes are nearly always comforting and, in medical literature, are said always to be so. I only hesitate because the only other patient of mine who reported sighting her husband was one who was not comforted. Again, I had attended the family for some years and I knew that the husband was extremely worried about the possibility of predeceasing his wife.

"She is unable to handle money," he had told me, and he amassed huge savings for her in case he did die first. He knew he had a heart condition, which might carry him off suddenly, and one day it did. After his death his fears were shown to be all too well founded. Overwhelmed by his provision she set about spending it. She told me that she was troubled by seeing her husband standing looking frowningly at her in the place where he always used to stand.

Unfortunately she redecorated her house completely to try to prevent this recurring, presumably by making the place less familiar to him, and so she did what he had feared, frittered her money away. She then sold the house and went away so I lost touch with her but I felt that her experience was perhaps closer to a hallucination from a guilty conscience than a true after-death experience.

9

ANXIETY DREAMS

What are anxiety dreams?

Anxiety dreams are without doubt the most common dreams that you remember when you wake. If you like, they are the detritus from your daytime memories that cannot be sorted by your brain in REM sleep. They are unable to be filed away in memory so are thrown back into your waking mind.

''Do something to make this feeling softer, less hurtful, less worrying or less upsetting to your mind so that it may be placed in store,'' is what your dreaming brain is saying and it colours the picture with emotive material so that when you wake it has a chance of not being forgotten as casual dreams are.

My anxiety dream

I woke this morning having dreamed that I was in Chengdu on holiday in a featureless concrete hotel. My husband was with me and a host of other younger relatives. We were at the end of our vacation and trying to get ready to go home. I wanted to find some clean and attractive bathing facilities for my daughter-in-law and her child before we left and my husband came in to our bleak room to tell me that he had arranged this with the management. Somehow I was then on a bicycle travelling on dirt roads between tropical trees, not a forest. It was not threatening. It was uphill and hard work and the roads were winding. I was looking for my daughter-in-law to tell her it was time to go home. She always seemed to be just too far ahead to call to and I pedalled on in the hope of catching up. It all appeared to be becoming too difficult. I was getting further away from the hotel by the minute and we had to meet a deadline for going home. I then woke.

The punch line was that it was all becoming too difficult. I could accept that. I look after the grandchildren on certain days but I was going on holiday to Sikkim and it was going to be difficult for my daughter and daughter-in-law to cope with the days I was leaving them with, for they were committed to their work and would now have to seek a stopgap. My holidays, while I look forward to them, have recently been less than healthy, both my husband and I coming back from Mexico with chest infections which were not improved by the long flights or the long journeys within the country. Chengdu, for me, has always been a place of bleak memory as it is where I returned to from Tibet, still suffering the effects of mountain sickness, and the hotel there, with its comfortless echoing halls which seemed to go on forever, is always anxiety-producing.

So this was just a mild dream, related to my forthcoming holiday and my anxieties about leaving my grandmotherly duties, with just a dash of wondering how I would be feeling when I returned from this particular sortie into the wild blue yonder. It was a very simple dream.

What causes an anxiety dream?

You may be worried about something, the anxious rat running round a trap sort of worry that starts as soon as you go to bed and switch the light off. These worries stop you getting to sleep in the first place and for that there are relaxation techniques. One technique is to think about your worry and make a decision about it earlier in the evening. Even if the decision is to look at your problem in depth the next day then that seems to leave your mind content and allow sleep to come.

Dealing with anxiety dreams

I have been keeping a dream diary and thinking out my problems from day to day, and this has led to my dreams becoming far more explicable because they are no longer a mishmash of long held anxieties. I have dealt with them. My dreams are now mostly up-to-the-minute problems and so a great deal easier to analyse.

This is something you will find. To begin with, your dreams will have a great deal of conflicting feelings and material in them. Tease out the strongest feeling, find its origin, and deal with it. The next night will have another problem, maybe, but as you deal with your anxieties in this way you will come to a much simpler form of dreaming where morning after morning your dreams show you the things that really upset you.

In another technique, you write down your worries on a piece of paper and put them by your bed to look at when you wake. Again that usually allows sleep to come. What it does not always do is pacify your dreaming brain which is quite likely to produce anxiety dreams that you wake to. To cure the dreams you need to settle down and sort your lifestyle out so that the anxiety is dispersed.

Debt anxieties

Perhaps you have spent too much money and are short of cash? Perhaps you have been left without enough money for your daily needs; for instance, if you have a young family you have no ability to get out and earn more? You feel trapped. Your daytime state of mind is full of anxiety. Should you sell your house? Where should you go for help? What should you do?

Your dreams are going to be full of insoluble problems that you struggle against. You may dream that you are walking through an empty house when you suddenly find you are in a room with no doors and can't get out. You shout but no one hears. You have to try to find the way you came in by but it appears to have disappeared. Other friends drop by to tell you that they are fine. They seem to be able to come and go at will. You can't. Then you wake.

For instance, I had a patient who bought herself a huge new family four-wheel drive vehicle, getting a large loan to do so. Within months she found she could not pay the interest on her loan, let alone the money she needed to add in so that she could slowly pay back the loan.

She became very anxious and at that time her dreams were all about struggling through tropical jungles with a machete which turned into a blunt table knife. She was trailing her children along and there seemed to be more of them than she actually had because their school friends had come along for the outing and she had nothing to feed them. They had tried to take a shortcut to the shops and the jungle had closed in on them.

She woke exhausted with the effort. Nearly every night she suffered that sort of dream. Then she became depressed and her dreams became flatter and she slept less and became even more tired.

She eventually took my advice to go to the Citizens' Advice Bureau for legal help. They helped her to get free legal advice, which led her to sell the car and pay back the money with the help of a small loan from her parents, and she began to see daylight. Her sleep became less punitive and longer. She did not require medication and gradually she became employed, solvent and free from anxiety dreams.

Deadline anxieties

Simple anxiety dreams brought on by looming deadlines abound. Everyone knows the frisson of pre-examination nerves. Professionals who have spent years sitting examinations usually find themselves in an examination hall of some kind and things start to go wrong.

Here is one dream I was told of: "I dreamed that a neurologist was doing an extremely complex set of tests on me, which seemed like an intelligence test. I started off well, but as time went on a crowd of about a dozen people in the room, who were chattering and pottering around, began trying harder and harder to distract me. I said I hoped there wasn't a time limit for the test because I was beginning to be slowed down by the distractions and was having difficulties filling in a list of similes linking the words 'disillusioned' and 'disappointed'. Then one of the chatty observers turned to another man and said, 'Professor, when I was helping you to set this up, did you not tell me it had to be done in a certain time and that means that there is now only three minutes to finish the paper?' The Professor agreed! I was horror struck and started to try to work faster but in my mind I thought, 'I expect my reaction to this unexpected stress is part of the test.' "

That is the sort of dream I get when I have had a day that starts with a packed surgery, followed by house calls that go on and on with messages reaching me to do yet another one, while I know that an evening surgery looms and I had promised to collect the children from school, and I know there is no food in the house so have to fit in shopping somewhere, especially as friends are coming to stay the next day. Just a usual bad day for a doctor with a family, followed by an anxiety dream!

Guilt

Guilt is another emotion that triggers uncomfortable dreams. One night I dreamed I was in my best friend's house. It is a magnificent place that is more like an antique exhibition than an everyday house because she and her husband are both very artistic and collect beautiful china. It has always amazed me how they managed to keep such a place and bring up four children, while my house is being distressed by the minute by mine. So I was standing there and the corridor had become very narrow so that, as I turned, my coat began to catch on the furniture and the ornaments wobbled. I was very anxious and stood very still but I wanted to go to the toilet and had to go there extremely carefully so as not to knock anything over. It took me a long time and when I came out I felt awfully guilty because she had arrived with a friend and they were both desperate to get into the bathroom and I realised that I had been keeping them out. I picked up my gloves and noticed I had brought two odd ones. The other ladies looked at me and I felt mortified. They told me I had missed the antique sale they had just been to. I had clearly arranged to meet them there so felt guilty about that and began to apologise. Then they said they had bought a beautiful mirror and I could advise them where to hang it. I looked around and there seemed nowhere to put it – I had no good ideas and seemed to be disappointing them all down the line.

I woke then, thankful it was a dream. Now that dream would mean little to an analyst but I was well aware of its significance to me. During the week prior to the dream I had begun to realise that I had immersed myself in my own work and had not even telephoned good friends with whom I usually kept in touch. My friend was one such and she had been unwell and I had not continued to ask how she was doing. There were other friends who had asked me out to their houses and it was now months later and I had not reciprocated. I felt very guilty and very much remiss. The dream merely highlighted my very appropriate mounting guilt. The morning after, I determined to fulfil a few social and caring obligations. I phoned to make plans to meet all the people to whom I owed a visit, and I slept peacefully that night. My mind had eventually decided that, however committed I was to my own daily tasks, caring for my friends had escalated in my thoughts until not doing it had wrecked my peace of mind. It was not a serious guilt. It was however there and my dreams brought it to the fore quite neatly.

Bigger feelings of guilt give more anxious dreams, but there is always material to show you where they come from and your conscience does the rest.

Incidentally, my dream also had intrinsic factors in it. Needing the toilet was in fact a need when I woke. Dreams will mix material. You have to learn to look at all the bits and see where they come from and discard the inessentials.

Dreams of pursuit

You may have dreams that show you that you are very anxious to get to something. Is it a job you aspire to? Is it a scholarship you are in competition for?

A young friend of mine who very much enjoys making model aeroplanes and has a great collection was also in competition for a music scholarship. He had been practising incredibly hard for the examination and was really committed to the work. He was playing, I was assured, as well as he possibly could.

One night just before the exam he dreamed he was putting together an extremely rare model aeroplane. It was all going well and when he had finished he was delighted with the result and sat back to admire it. He said he put his whole collection together around this new addition and it looked very fine. Then, suddenly, the new one took off and started to fly round the room. The window was open and he was terrified it would fly away. As he leapt after it others took off and he was leaping and shouting to them to come in to land. He said he was quite glad to wake up. Chasing them was hard work.

"Could be you have an idea of what it is you are chasing?"

I said. ''Could be,'' he smiled at me. He did not need me to tell him the meaning.

Being pursued is usually a less pleasant dream. The desire to escape tends to be precipitated by being under too much pressure at work or in your home. This is a major threat to peace of mind and your brain lets you know about it in no uncertain fashion. It is really one step less than a nightmare and you wake with haunting memories of being hunted by savages, who you know are cannibals, or by men with guns who are trying to shoot you. Often the place, or the names of the hunters, or what they look like, gives you a clue to where your loss of peace of mind comes from.

Chasing trains that are just leaving, racing after friends who have gone on ahead and being told your work is just not good enough are all anxiety dreams.

Confused anxieties

A friend who has a very active five year old and two other children, as well as a job and a house, fell asleep after a particularly bad day when she felt too ill to function properly. She dreamed that she was toiling up the stairs to her house with huge bags of shopping and, when she got in to the house, she saw that the five year old had torn all the radiators off the walls and the mess in the house was terrible.

She said she just stood there and said to herself. ''I don't even know where to start now. I can't go on.'' Then she woke. In fact she felt a bit better and was thankful to notice that her house was intact and the children were well asleep. The material for the dream had come from a problem she had had with a leaking radiator in the bathroom a week previously. It had not been a major difficulty, but had caused her quite a bit of anxiety at the time as she was not sure how serious it was at first. Only she was in a good position to interpret that dream. It was simple for her and she realised she needed more help and organised things so she got it.

Keeping an eye on anxiety dreams

This dialogue between your dreaming brain and your waking self is useful and a good way of being sure that you have a quiet mind and conscience. A patient who knew I was interested in dreams, and had come to the conclusion that keeping a dream diary might be interesting, came to me with a couple of dreams she had had on consecutive nights.

She had a son whose children she helped to look after and had just been told that his wife was going to have another child.

The first night she dreamed that she was bathing a very new baby and had been left in full charge of it, though she hoped the mother might arrive at any moment. A woman came into the room who appeared to be the mother and said that there had been a bad accident involving her son. She was devastated. The woman asked her what she thought about the news.

"I said that I could not contemplate my son predeceasing me," she told me. "I said to this woman that if I was never to see him again I would just pretend he was in the next room or away on a holiday. I could not face any other possibility. Then I woke and I was still shaking at the thought hours later."

"What do you think that means?" I asked her.

"I usually am in contact with my son every week, if not every few days, but he had been away on out-of-town jobs and I had been busy at home, too busy to give time to going to see him. His wife just drops the children at my house and collects them again. I felt that my dream was telling me that my feelings for my son were stronger than any other feeling and I was a fool not to be in contact with him. I was only looking after his children because I loved him."

"Then what happened?" I asked

"The next night I dreamed that I was looking after his children and they were not well and I was doing my best to keep them comfortable in the way I used to do with my son when he was ill. But they seemed to get worse and worse, until their mother came for them when they all just got better and went home, leaving me exhausted, and then I woke.''

''So?''

''So I felt it was a sequel to the night before and my dream told me that I should not try to be my grandchildren's mother. I was just their gran and my real tie of love was with my son and I should not waste the time we could have together but enjoy what he could give me. At the end of those two dreams I felt happy about doing just what I was doing, but not offering any more or expecting the kids to think of me as anything more than a nanny, and I decided to make a regular half hour every week when I could chat to my son on the phone if he was free. Since then, those sorts of dreams have not recurred so I knew I was right about their meaning.''

I do not think anyone but my patient herself could have come to those decisions, but she was sure about them and certainly her dreams stopped which is always a sign of the return of peace of mind.

Inadequacy anxieties

Dreams of inadequacy often involve you in finding yourself in an embarrassing situation, but the situation tends to show whether the inadequacy stems from your home or work.

Here is a dream where there was clearly a work stress situation: ''I was in a new office in a strange open plan workspace full of computers. Nothing was connected up, but it seemed to me that, although I would have liked a computer terminal and desk by the picture window, the special plug sockets were all away from the light at the other side of the room. This was a pity because the view from the window was spectacular, including an artificial pond or perhaps a flooded garden, and beyond it was the sweep of a broad river. As time went on I first found that I had no shoes on; then as my secretary started talking about the trials of living with an alcoholic husband, and as other people started taking part in the conversation I found myself in a bed, which had suddenly appeared in the room, and I found I had no clothes on. They all turned to me expecting me to get up and fix the computers for them. I woke wondering how I was going to extricate myself from that position.''

Finding yourself naked

Dreams of finding yourself naked or improperly dressed among crowds are, I believe, one of general insecurity. The crowds often do not notice your predicament. Within the dream it is your unhappy reaction that matters and you should look at your feelings to interpret the dream. Is the ambience of your dream at work or in the home? Did you know anyone in the watching crowd and were you generally upset or was it the opinion of a single person that caused you anxiety? You are clearly worried about not measuring up to your own or someone else's expectations. Explore the possibilities in your waking mind as it is a situation that you may well be able to alleviate by further learning or experience, and starting the process will stop that sort of dream.

Frustration

Dreams of frustration could be of pushing heavy objects into position and never quite managing. You might also dream of trying to put tiny pieces of jigsaw together or mending a precious vase that you have smashed and not managing to make any of the pieces fit together.

Signs of trouble brewing

The Senoi, a small tribe in Malaysia who lived in a circumscribed community in the years before the Second World War dispersed them into a larger population, believed that dreams were a mirror of existing events and a pointer to the future. If one of them dreamed that he had quarrelled with his best friend he would feel that this meant that there was unconscious conflict beginning to arise in his mind that would burst out into the tribal circle. He would discuss this dream with his family and with his friend, and would then give his friend a present to ward off the clouding of the relationship. The dreamer would then try to dream a lucid dream about being at peace with his friend to cement the reinstatement of goodwill.

It is not a bad idea to look at your nightly dreams to check if there is trouble brewing in your state of mind and do something about it sooner rather than later.

Dreaming in old age

It is generally said that as you get older your dreaming diminishes. Many people have conducted research projects to prove this. There is also a general idea that in old age dreams tend to be sad ones of anxiety and loss.

This may be so to some extent, but I believe that as you get older you begin to ignore your dreams and so you forget the ones you wake to. Keep a dream diary and you will be surprised how you suddenly seem to have started dreaming again. In youth there are so many extraordinary happenings that your dreams are bound to be more bizarre than in old age. As you get older your lifestyle becomes more settled and there is not so much to upset your peace of mind.

Anxiety dreams from work stress will disappear when you retire. At the same time, for many people, old age is a time of financial retrenchment. Your pension is seldom as good as your salary and there are few trips and excitements of the work-engendered sort. You may have anxiety dreams about making your income meet your expenditure instead.

I do not believe you dream of yourself in old age as tired and incapable, unless your dreaming brain is trying to show you that your health is failing and you are not as active or well as you ought to be. If you do dream repeatedly of feeling unwell and unable I think it is time for you to go to get a physical check up.

I am sure that in old age, if you suddenly seem to stop dreaming and your sleep becomes attenuated, you might begin to wonder if you are not becoming depressed and seek professional advice.

Mostly as you get older you dream of yourself as able to run as fast, think as quick, be as attractive as you used to be. In fact, you seldom really see yourself in dreams. You are there and active in the dream but you are not looking at yourself so your age does not matter. All the kinds of dreams that you used to be prone to in youth may visit you if there is occasion for this to happen. It is just not quite so likely that you are engaged in the sexual mix and match of adolescence and youth, the family anxieties of middle age and the work problems of employment.

You can still get a great deal of interest and useful information from a dream diary and as it goes on you may be able to trace anxieties that should be resolved before they become chronic.

Dreams tend to simplify if you look at their meaning regularly and do something about it. This is especially true of anxiety dreams in the older person. At first the dream seems too complicated to tease out the different strands but if you manage to get even one daytime anxiety pinpointed and then dealt with, you will find that the next night's dream is that much simpler to unravel.

Acting upon anxiety dreams

It is important to get the dialogue going between your waking brain and your dreaming brain that I described earlier. This is, I believe, what should be normal for everyone.

Ignoring your dreams is wasting a process that is a normal

part of your body function. Some people dream very little or remember very little of what they dream. That is normal for them and part of the way that they are made, or how they have become perhaps because of taking medication, smoking, or some such dream attenuating habit.

If you dream, and especially if you are able to remember your dream because it left a marked impression on your waking mind, that dream was thrown out of your dream sorting mechanism to be analysed by you and acted on by day so that the memory can be stored as soon as possible and your mind brought back to the peaceful state where you are not anxious, guilty, resentful or apprehensive.

These worrying emotions are harmful even to your waking self. They nag away at you and prevent you giving your whole mind to your daily work. However, by day you seldom think of clearing your mind of irritants. It takes your dreaming brain at night to highlight your problems. If you learn to listen to it your sleep will be more restful.

Waking after an anxiety dream does not allow you to greet the day as if you have had a good sleep and feel refreshed. Usually you feel shattered by the effort of running away or hiding or battling or whatever emotion your dream has been highlighting. You do not wake comfortable. Your dreaming brain does not want you to. It wants you to sort out whatever is at the root of your lack of peace of mind. Too many anxieties unsolved and you will get a nightmare and that is something to be avoided if at all possible.

Equally your dreaming brain is hard at work trying to soften your worries or guilt. "Sleep on it" is time-honoured advice. I had a friend who used to use the phrase repeatedly as an answer to any problem. "What happens if you sleep on it and you have no answers?" I asked him once. "I sleep on it again," was his reply, "and again and again until an answer does appear."

Your dreaming brain does try to soften those memories and

thoughts it cannot file. Insoluble guilt or sorrow or anxiety do imperceptibly become less acute with time and sleep. Your brain in dream sleep keeps on trying to achieve peace of mind for you. A bit of help from your waking brain does no harm.

10

COMMON DREAMS

Flying

Flying is a dream that is common to everyone. I was speaking to a financier one evening and asked him if he had ever flown in a dream. He was used to travelling all over the world by plane and misunderstood me, saying, "No, if possible, I reserve my flying for day time." When I explained, he nodded, "You mean levitation. I often whisk over the country about two feet off the ground in dreams. It is a great feeling."

In fact, nearly all dreams of flying are attractive dreams. They facilitate movement, allow you to speed from one place to the next at great speed, without knocking into anything. You seldom seem to fly high in the air, as aeroplanes do. The most I have heard of or experienced is of zooming along about tree height, or soaring like a bird flying between hills at hilltop level.

I used to dream of superb flights swooping around Arthur's Seat, a 500m hill in the middle of Edinburgh. It is the remnant of volcanic activity so is now a jagged stony height with a spreading green carpet of rough grass and whin that runs down steep slopes and along great lengths of flat surface. Flying there was a great delight. I swooped and turned and trailed incredibly beautiful garments of gold and silver, rather like a Chinese dragon kite, and in fact the dream may have come from some sighting of that sort of thing because people do fly kites in that area and I love watching the movement against the sky.

Freud never had a dream of flying. He did once treat a very short woman patient whose dreams of flying just above the ground he put down to a wish fulfilment of wanting to see above other people for once. This may have been her motivation. It could not have been that of my financier friend who is a very tall man and has never found difficulty seeing a rugby match from even the last row of the crowd.

I believe it may be a wish to move freely and without constraint rather than a wish for height. As for the dreamers who swoop about in the air, their dreams are very common in adolescence and clearly offer escape and freedom of movement and may well be wishes of emancipation as adolescence, more than all ages, is a time when there is a growing wish for independence.

Adolescence is also a time of burgeoning sexual desire, a wish to love and be loved and a need to look for these things. It is a time of intense ambition in every field and the soaring freedom of flight may have something to do with the show-off feeling that ambition fosters.

I always thought that my dreams of flying, which occurred at a time when I was burdened by four young children, a busy house to keep and part-time work to sustain, was without doubt a time when my dreaming brain ran free, unfettered by home ties, and my grotty day time clothes were transformed into the sort of thing I felt like wearing. There is no fear, no vertigo, just delight and extroversion.

Dreams of flying often start by stepping off a high point or leaping into the air, somewhat like Superman, and there is a primary trepidation until you realise you can stay in the air without a problem. Then it becomes all pleasure until you land, and that too is without difficulty and leads to waking.

Freud was worried by these dreams as he felt you had to

have experienced the feeling before you dreamed it. He suggested that it was the feeling of being thrown and caught in your parent's arms as a baby and so, he suggested, these dreams were a form of infantile love. He also noted that they might be the same feeling as being on a swing. I believe they have a great deal more in common with the freedom you feel in water where water ballet has very much the same quality. Not everyone has performed this, or indeed swam, but just watching kites flying in freedom can give you the same feeling. I think the dream is motivated by the energetic feeling of well being in someone whose ambition is running free and who wants to be noticed.

Waking with a jerk

Dreams where you wake with a jerk of your whole body are almost certainly just a mistiming of the release of muscle paralysis normal in REM sleep. This is usually a smooth process where your sleep lightens so you are in non-REM sleep before you wake, but if you wake into the end of REM sleep your muscle movement may have to hurry to switch on and you feel the enervation entering your musculature with a jerk. Sometimes you wake unable to move and feel panic. There is no need to. Lie quietly and movement returns in a couple of seconds. The story from the Middle Ages that your soul is returning to your body in a hurry may be attractive but is not credible.

Phallic symbols

Freud suggested that all objects within dreams can be translated into male or female images seen in childhood and remembered. All pointed objects he associated with the penis, and all smooth round objects with female breasts. This view has persisted in common beliefs, and in some cases it may be true. But objects also have very clear tribal and ethnic associations as well as personal ones, built up by your own experiences, and these you should look for and use to help you interpret your dreams.

Eastern interpretation of common dreams

Tibetan doctors are interested in their patients' dreams. Buddhist monks passed down teachings through the ages in the form of written documents called the "Tantra of Secret Instructions on the Eight Branches, the Essence of the Elixir of Immortality". This is more usually referred to as the "Four Tantras". These writings, which may have been composed as early as the ninth century AD were edited in about 1688 and illustrated with beautiful paintings. It has become a medical text called the "Blue Beryl" and within it are described the ways to interpret dreams. For instance, dreaming that a bird is sitting on your head is a grave prognostic sign. Doctors are instructed to warn the relatives that his patient may die.

If I dreamed that a bird was sitting on my head I should consider that it might mean that my hair had got tangled and was pulling, an extrinsic stimulus, or that I was anxious about my hair falling out or getting thin on top. If the bird pecked me I should wake thinking that I had a boil forming at the spot, perhaps, or was it a headache? At no time would I consider it of grave prognostic significance.

But in Tibet, it is the custom to leave dead bodies exposed for the vultures to eat the flesh away and so dispose of the corpse. They do not bury their dead because the ground is so stony and unmalleable that graveyards would be difficult to make. This way the birds are fed, and the dead person made into hygienic bones in no time. It is their preferred technique following death. You can readily see why, for them, dreaming of a bird on their heads is an omen of trouble ahead at the very least. This is an ethnic dream which is particular to, and significant for, a seriously ill Tibetan. In Europe, doctors would be equally anxious if their very ill patient reported dreams of going to his own funeral. Each ethnic community has specialised dreams and someone from that community is best placed to be able to interpret them.

Personal and culturally-specific interpretations

In the same way, you build up personal pictures that mean something quite specific to you and you should learn to isolate these pictures and be aware of them, as they are useful signs of what your dreaming mind is trying to tell you.

Take snakes for instance. Talk about dreaming of a snake and everyone tells you that you were dreaming of a sexual contact. That may be true for some people but I met a girl who, when I told her I was researching material about dreams, said, ''When I dream of snakes it means that my supervisor is going to be, or has been, particularly beastly to me.''

She explained that being in the media business meant that she had to work to deadlines and her immediate supervisor was, she felt, unreasonable and hostile. She had had several dreams of snakes writhing about her and had woken upset by them. At the time she was happily married to a man she loved and she told him about her dreams because they were troubling her. She said she could not understand why, when she was so happy sexually and in his love, that she was dreaming these terrible dreams. It was he, she told me, who had appreciated that these dreams followed evenings when she had come in saying that her supervisor had been completely impossible and was trying to get her fired. Once she realised what her dream meant she used to walk extremely warily for a few days after dreaming of snakes and, she said, she felt it had helped her to keep her job.

''Why do you think snakes are so dreadful?'' I asked her. ''I come from India and I was brought up to think of snakes as very threatening, frightening creatures with the power of death. I cannot change that. I have never thought of them in any sexual context. That would seem ridiculous to me. It was the other people at work who told me they were sexual objects.''

I was interested because I also was brought up in an Asian country so I also think of snakes with fear and distress and associate dreaming of them with trouble. In fact, when I dream of snakes I know that someone is bad-mouthing me behind my back and it will mean difficulties at work, so I go in and, just as the girl did, I walk warily until I find out what is going on and right it by holding a meeting, sorting things out, apologising if I have been heavy handed, or staying well clear of the person seeking my mortification until the episode is past. For me, many snakes or huge snakes mean a large problem. A glimpse of snakes signifies a small one. My dreams are as specific as that.

I dreamed recently of being out with a grandchild when a large plastic light green snake rattled past and then turned on me, its fangs showing. ''Just love it a bit more and it will disappear,'' said my companion so I did and it curled up in my arms very like my yellow Burmese cat whose eyes were the same colour as the snake's, and whose wide yawn was identical to the toothy one that I had faced from my snake.

Now, I knew that I was going out that night with people, one of whom was giving me a hard time at work because I had suggested that he had not done his job correctly. I did not need the dream to tell me to walk warily and be extra polite. It was a mixed dream because the snake, which really turned out to be my cat, did need extra loving. He is a very companionable cat and likes to be with me. But when I am at home and working at the computer, I shut him out of the room and he hates it. Equally, when he is in the room he sits on the keyboard and I hate that. But my dream was telling me I was not looking after him as I should and my conscience agreed with my dream so I took him for a walk in the garden and petted him all evening and the dream did not recur.

In a way, these ethnic and particular dreams are the reason

that dream dictionaries gained credence. They put meanings to objects that everyone in a community placed a similar meaning to. Your dreams may include material that is stereotypical to your race or particular to you. Any repetition of a dream object is worth looking closely at to see if the same circumstances are precipitating it. It may then act as a dream of advance warning.

11

DRUG INDUCED DREAMS

Dreams are very sensitive to the foods you eat and scents you smell, as well as to herbs and medicines. These things also affect your sleep pattern, some increasing dream sleep, some preventing it. Where dream sleep is suppressed, it seems to resurface or break through after a week or two, and then your dreams may be quite wild, as if your dreaming brain is having to make up for lost time. When you stop medication that suppresses dream sleep, the same thing happens and you spend longer in REM sleep than normal. This appears entirely rational if you believe that REM sleep is the time when your brain is sorting your memories.

The beta-blocker group of drugs

These are usually used to treat high blood pressure and angina. They often cause nightmares, especially the fat soluble (lipophylic) members of the group. They may also cause disturbed sleep with a tendency to wake often. In small doses these beta-blockers are also offered to patients to treat anxiety and, though the medication may steady its takers by day, it may exacerbate their dreaming by night. As the dose increases, however, these medicines suppress REM sleep and so dreams are at first prevented and then gradually spill over into your sleep. If you changed your medication to a different group of medicines to treat high blood pressure or angina, your dreams would return in a cascade of night-time fantasies that would again give you disturbed sleep until things settled down and you had made up your dream time.

This desire of your brain to make up on REM sleep, and so make up on dreamtime after it has been suppressed, is the clearest sign that dreams are essential to your brain. It happens after you stop any drug that prevents REM sleep. It is clear that your brain is working hard during this part of sleep. It resents any suppression of activity and tries to make it up as soon as possible.

Amphetamines

Amphetamines decrease the amount of REM sleep and dreaming you normally have. They also tend to keep you from falling asleep. Ecstasy is of this family of drugs and completely suppresses REM sleep, so for this reason alone must be said to be harmful to those who take it.

Caffeine, however, which is also a stimulant substance found in tea, coffee, and some fizzy drinks, has little effect on REM sleep or dreams, although taken at night it may tend to keep you awake.

Anti-histamines

Some anti-histamines suppress REM sleep so if you are on this sort of medication for hay fever you may notice that you lose your dreams while you are on them and, when you stop, your dreams may be quite troubling for a week or two. Some antihistamines are sold over the counter as sleep aids. These may have the same effect.

Sleeping pills

The big anxiolytic family of benzodiazepines all suppress REM sleep and dreaming. As part of their immediate anxiolytic effect they will stop your anxiety dreams for a short while. This may give you time to work out your problems so that, even if you get more dreaming on stopping them, they may not be upsetting dreams because you have reached peace of mind. If you continue to take benzodiazepines you will find that a few dreams begin to break through again. You will, however, still face disturbed sleep for some nights when you stop them.

Temazepam is a member of the benzodiazepines. It is a well-known sleeping pill and is widely used. It does suppress dreams. This may not be a bad thing in all cases.

If you are having repetitive nightmares, some nights of peace from them, coupled with a good sleep, may be enough to allow you to work out the cause and prevent it recurring. In addition, seriously ill people occasionally have dreadful dreams. I remember a very ill lady telling me that she dreamed she was on her knees in the snow in front of a snowplough that came on inexorably. She could do nothing about it. She felt too weak to move. She felt very frightened. Miserable dreams like this that mirror the clinical condition should not be tolerated. Even a small nightly dose of temazepam would prevent their recurrence.

There are sleeping pills that do not change your sleeping pattern. These are to be preferred when getting to sleep is a problem and dreaming is not. Examples of these are Zimovane (zopiclone), Stilnoct (zolpidem), and Sonata (zaleplon), which are now commonly prescribed in most countries. They have no effect on dream sleep so there is no rebound of disturbed dreams when you stop taking them.

Anti-depressants

Many anti-depressant medications, especially the sedative ones that need to be taken at night, suppress REM sleep and dreaming. If you miss your night-time fantasies you can ask your doctor to prescribe an antidepressant that does not take away your dreams. In depression your dreams become flat, infrequent and sad, and one sign that you are beginning to improve is when your dreaming increases and becomes florid again.

Alcohol

Alcohol decreases REM sleep and dreaming in the first half of the night but in the second half, if you have drunk more than a little, you may suffer increased dreaming and disturbed sleep. Alcoholics who stop drinking suddenly may face a sudden increase in dream disturbed sleep and may even go on to have hallucinations and delirium by day.

Nicotine

Smokers have few dreams. Nicotine suppresses dream sleep. Regular smokers must get some dream break-through, but their dreams seem attenuated or only occur when some monumental happening in their lives spills over into sleep. Disturbed dreaming follows abstinence from tobacco as REM sleep is made up, but occasional dreams of deprivation from smoking may persist for years. Smokers miss the night-time give and take between daytime feelings and night-time dreams that I feel is a natural and useful body mechanism.

Steroids

Steroids reduce REM sleep and dreaming. Asthmatics who are put on short courses of steroids may sleep deeply as a result. As their dose is prescribed to reduce gradually, they may not suffer a period of dream disturbance when they stop.

Pain killers

Opiates are strong painkillers and sleep producing medication. When first given they may suppress REM sleep but if taken regularly their effect on this sleep stage tails off and dreams return in an almost normal fashion.

Aspirin and paracetemol have no effect on dreaming or REM sleep.

Drugs which produce nightmares

Some medication, such as the levodopa derivatives that are used to treat Parkinson's disease, as well as baclofen, which is a muscle relaxant, have the ability to precipitate nightmares that do not wear off, so the medication needs to be changed to allow the taker a reasonable night. One of my patients who was taking baclofen because he suffered the muscle spasms of multiple sclerosis reported that, when he started the medication, it did relax his muscle spasm but he started having nightmares. These were so severe that he woke from a terrible dream and, turning over, went back to sleep to be engulfed in the same nightmare which just powered on as if it had never stopped. I found an alternative medication for him, which gave him similar muscle relaxation without bad dreams. Other people get no bad dreams from the same medication. It appears to be a personal reaction.

Reports I read in medical journals suggested that mefloquine, a commonly used anti-malarial medication, could cause increased dream activity and disturbed sleep. As this is often taken by tourists entering malaria infested countries as a prophylactic, there may be many people who think that their dreams and poor sleep were due to the holiday, the food or anxiety, when in fact the cause could just have been their anti-malaria pill.

Any medication that either stops dreaming or causes bad dreams is a cause for concern and should be reported to your doctor so that he may change it for something that gives you normal sleep.

Alternative remedies for nightmares

Homeopaths suggest that nux vomica, aconite or ignatia prevent the disturbed sleep that is associated with nightmares. However, to use these correctly you really need to see a trained homeopath who can advise you.

Modern herbalists no longer emphasise the need to prevent

dreaming and mostly concentrate on offering herbs that encourage sleep. Passion flower, hibiscus, camomile, valerian and lime flower teas are some of the tisanes they recommend and many of these may be found in supermarkets and chemists. However, if you suddenly begin to dream more, or if you find your dreams have deserted you after starting one of these herbal teas, consider stopping them and see if your dreams return to normal. If you then re-try your herbal drink at night and your dreams disappear again or again become florid, you will know that it is the tisane that is having an effect on your sleep pattern and you will be able to use it appropriately.

I have heard reports of increased dreaming with most of these herbs but just as personal reactions, not universally. They may affect different people in different ways. I know that in France I began to dream in a very florid manner. I could not think why but in the end traced it to a butcher's sausage which had a high quantity of nutmeg or mace, a herb I scarcely ever use at home.

It is an interesting experiment to try out various herbs and spices in your cooking and see what effect they have on your dreaming. Herbs are taste stimulants but they are also a great deal more than that as the doctors of long ago knew well.

Aromatherapists suggest that narcissus, mimosa and cedar-wood scents increase dreaming. I must confess I did dream very freely when I was last in Madeira, walking by day in the mimosa groves. I had previously put it down to the different food but it could have been those lovely yellow flowers.

Food and drink

Any food or drink may have an effect on your sleep. Little research has been done on the effect of food and drink on your dreaming. Cheese is said to encourage dreams, as well as red wine and chocolate.

12

THE RIGHT WAY TO INTERPRET ALL THESE DREAMS

You are the only person who can really interpret your dreams and have any idea of their significance or importance. In addition, much of your dreaming material is very private to you and you do not want other people prying. You may not want to bare your soul to your analyst or your friends who tell you they understand how to make sense of your dreams.

So how do you set about interpreting your dreams on a day-to-day basis to help you with your normal daily life?

Remembering dreams

First go over your dream when you wake. Try to remember as much of it as you can and, if you have a problem with that, write down the salient facts. In the middle of the night note down enough to remind you of the dream. You can then turn over and go back to sleep. The time to mull it over is in the morning at your convenience.

The best time to get the full flavour of a dream is when you wake with time to spare and can lie and go over your dream then and there. Your emotions are fresh and clear and are still quite strong within you. This is fine if it occurs in that last part of the night when you are approaching the time to get up. It is not sensible in the middle of the night when you should be getting back to sleep to get the right amount of sleep for you to have a good day. Then you must just jot down a fact or two, clear your mind and turn over.

This is a very real problem as you get older. After about fifty, instead of going into Stage 1 and 2 non-REM sleep between more deep sleep and REM sleep, you tend to wake. This is annoying but natural as you get older. The trick is to get back to sleep as quickly as possible. If you have to go to the toilet, do it without waste of time. Do not let your daytime worries obtrude. Try repeating a simple word and concentrate on it. Try telling yourself a story that you use to gain sleep entry at the beginning of the night. Try counting sheep, but don't let yourself waken.

The trouble is that if you have woken to a dream you will forget it if you go right back to sleep. That is where a jotter by the bed is a necessity to a dream diary. Jot down a few words to remind you and put the whole thing out of your mind. You should be able to recall the dream when you wake.

This business of forgetting dreams is a very real hindrance to dream interpretation. Dreams are ephemeral, evanescent whiffs of consciousness. They appear so strong when you wake but you will lose them entirely if you do not go over them to reinforce them in your memory or record them on paper or tape. A visit to the toilet and you will not have a dream to figure out.

On the other hand, as you get used to running over your dreams you will find that they seem to become more and more obvious. Their meanings are clear and, as you sort out the troubling thoughts that threaten your peace of mind, the things that matter stand out. In addition, as you clear up long forgotten troublesome memories, your dreams become so much simpler as they only contain current problems and you reach the stage where there is a give and take between your working brain by day and your dreaming brain by night, which is how I believe it should be.

If you can keep a diary of your dreams with a note of what you thought they meant at the time it makes for fascinating reading and may help you to analyse a complicated dream which has similar features to one you dealt with previously.

Recognising emotions

The first thing to think about is what emotion you are left with when you wake. Is it anger, anxiety, frustration, fear, resentment, joy, peaceful remembrance, horror or a mixture of some of these or other feelings?

Once you have isolated the main feeling within your dream look into your waking lifestyle to see where that feeling stems from. You may have many things frustrating you or causing anxiety. Go over each of them and see if some of your dream pictures highlight a particular problem.

For instance, if you feel anger, who is it with whom you were angry the previous day? If you were angry with several people, who appears to be involved in the dream? Is it a dream of the work environment or home? Are there hints about the dress or behaviour of the person in the dream that remind you of someone whom you were angry with? Have you had a slow burning anger mounting for some days? Was there something to trigger this dream?

Dream scenery

You will find in each dream that a lot of the pictures come from something you have seen or done on the day previous to the dream. You may recognise scenes or people from a television show that you saw before you went to bed. I remember one of my dreams was played out in a dusty wilderness in bright sunshine after having watched a Western on television. I knew the scene was of no significance. It was just an easy picture, readily available. The meaning had to be in what was happening in that desert. You may meet people you met the day before. Again, they may just be 'extras' popped in to receive the message your brain is trying to get across.

Your brain storage system appears to pool recent experience and sights and leave them swilling around in a retrievable morass for about twenty-four hours. After that your mind appears to be sorting them and filing them and they are not so easily available for a day or two. You seldom seem to dream of things that you experienced in between about day two and day five prior to a dream. After that your memories again become available to your dreaming brain and it may show you pictures that go right back far into your childhood; so far, in fact, that you may not recognise where they come from.

Some of the things you do and see in your dreams may appear to be completely new. They seldom are. You do not dream what you have not experienced somewhere, either vicariously or in person. The memories may be a bit different, names of places and people are changed, but you can often remember where the memory came from.

Working through the dream's clues

The scene itself may be coincidental, though you should look at it in case it helps you isolate your problem. For instance, you might find yourself on a beach shouting at a stranger who has stolen your picnic. He tells you his name is Tony, but you don't care. You wake from screaming at him full force and there is no doubt that you feel the desire to shout at someone.

The previous day you were at the hairdressers and your coiffeur cut your hair expensively but not well and not as you instructed. Looking back at the feeling in your dream you will recognise your angry frustration when you looked in the mirror. At that time you did not feel you could make a fuss, so you bottled your fury and left. Your unrelieved anger, however, remains and has shown up in your dream because it was so strong that your dreaming brain could not ameliorate it and soften it into peace of mind.

Why did you dream of a beach? Perhaps the hairdressers' salon was very warm and the lights were bright like sunshine. Looking back the feelings of the place were not dissimilar to those you experienced in your dream of the beach. What about Tony? Maybe there was a big poster on the wall of the hairdressers of a lady with a Toni perm. Perhaps even the sort of hairstyle you wanted? Certainly there are signs pushing you in the direction of your hairdressers even if you had not recognised the origin of your anger.

Acting upon your dreams' messages

So what do you do about it? Take a long look at your new hairstyle. Is it perhaps perfectly all right, if not what you wanted? Do you feel a bit foolish now and begin to feel glad that you have not made a fuss? Can you say to yourself, ''This style has possibilities and could be beautiful – I feel good about it now''? If not, and you still feel aggrieved, ring up your hairdresser and explain that you are unhappy with the result and ask him if he will rectify it as much as he is able without further cost. Both these courses will allow your venom to subside and you will sleep the easier for it.

This is a made-up dream but it shows the way dreams work to give you hints as well as leaving you with a feeling that needs your daytime attention. If you do not manage to give yourself relief from your slow burning anger, you will probably have another similar dream the next night, and so on until either your dreaming brain eventually manages to store the memory as time makes you forget, or you sort out the feeling by doing something about it by day.

Reaching acceptance or accepting an apology and restitution will give you peace of mind. Of course, if you sounded off in the hairdressers, causing a scene, and felt thoroughly ashamed about it, at night you might be left with such a feeling of embarrassment that you dream of losing your clothes at a party, and then you would have to come to terms with that emotion the next day instead.

Nullifying negative emotions

Hate, anger, guilt, resentment, stress, anxiety, sorrow and fear are all negative emotions. Overwhelmed by one of these, your dreaming brain may try to soften the emotion, but it will also highlight it by producing dreams that you wake to and notice.

Emotions like love, happiness, even ambition (if not tainted by stress and anxiety), do not upset your peace of mind in the same way. Your dreaming brain will not trouble you with these emotions, unless there are negative attachments such as jealousy or guilt attached to them.

Go over the subjects in each chapter in this book and consider whether your dream comes from any of these sources or a mix of them. To gain peace of mind you may have to discuss problems your dream has highlighted, settle emotional upsets, and change your lifestyle and approach to your family and work. Your dreams show you what is sticking in its mechanism. You have to think out how to remove that block by day.

Practical dream analysis

There is little point in delving too far in to each minuscule part of each dream. That way you will start making things up to fit the case. The main features of your dream are usually strong and obvious. After some months of regular dream analysis you will begin to find you have a sort of dialogue going between your day mind and your dreaming brain. Incidents by day are rapidly thrown back as dream pictures and minor upsets in your general peace of mind are highlighted. This is what I believe dreaming is there for. It is, in a way, another sense to help to keep you stable and content through life.

INDEX